FROM THE
GARDEN
TO THE
LAKES

FROM THE
GARDEN
TO THE
LAKES

By Glynis Gillespie

BROWN
DOG
BOOKS

Published under licence by Brown Dog Books and
The Self Publishing Partnership
7 Green Park Station, Bath BA1 1JB

www.selfpublishingpartnership.co.uk

ISBN printed book: 978-1-78545-034-1
ISBN e-book: 978-1-78545-035-8

Cover design by Kevin Rylands

Printed and bound by CPI Group (UK) Ltd, Croydon CR0 4YY

ACKNOWLEDGEMENTS

I would like to thank:

My gorgeous husband, John, for thinking up
the title of this book, and for just being my
gorgeous husband.

Jillo McNarry for suggesting that I write the book
in the first place.

All of my family, friends and workmates, for
putting up with me being an airhead while writing
this book.... Oh, wait a minute. I guess that's just
normal behaviour for me. I'll just thank them for
putting up with me then.

And

My mum and dad, as without them, this story
would not exist.

THANK YOU

CHAPTER 1

It was Monday the 18th of November 1957. The time was 17.00 and my mum Margaret Puddle went into labour. My dad Gerald had just arrived home from work and was greeted with the words, "Go and get the midwife." So, grabbing his bicycle, he cycled with ultimate speed in order to fetch her.

Earlier that day Mum had been told by the doctor to drink some castor oil and then have a bath. Hence at 19.50, when my mum's waters broke I slid into this world on a tidal wave, making my appearance with some urgency. There I was, bold as brass, and with a mop of bright auburn almost shoulder-length hair.

"What are you going to call her?" the doctor asked my mum when he arrived at my nana and grandad's house. My parents had lived since getting married on the 5th of January that same year.

"Glynis." my mum replied.

"Oh yes. That's very acceptable. Her initials will be GP, I like that," said the doctor.

I was born in my Nana's feather bed in Wellington Road, Gillingham, Kent, which is quite ironic really, seeing as my surname was going to be Puddle. Kent is known as the Garden of England and I am extremely proud to have been born there. Mum and Dad named me after Glynis Johns as she was their favourite film star. I figured it could have been worse, they could have been fans of the band Muddy Waters. I mean, growing up with the name Glynis Puddle was bad enough, but Muddy Puddle may well have brought on suicidal tendencies.

So, there we were living with Nana and Grandad. Nana worked in Featherstones a large departmental store where Mum had also worked before leaving to have me. Grandad was a bus driver. Dad's parents lived in the police flats over Chatham Dockyard as Grandad, after having been released after 25 years in the Royal Navy, joined the Navy police. Nana had worked in-service for aristocracy in a large hotel located just behind Buckingham Palace.

Living with Nana and Grandad was great, not that I can remember it being only a baby. However after I had turned six months old Mum and Dad decided it was time to move into our first family home in Stanley Road, Gillingham.

There were two incidents of abduction here. Mum went into a shop one day leaving me asleep in my pram outside, as mums did then. The first time, Mum came out of the shop to find an empty pram. Panic stricken she frantically looked up the road to see a woman carrying me away. She ran up to her grabbing me out of her arms.

"What do you think you're doing?" screamed Mum.

"She was crying, so I was just trying to get her back to sleep," said the abductor.

Mum didn't know whether to believe her, but gave her the benefit of the doubt anyway. The second time, again I was asleep outside a shop in my pram, when Mum came out to find me, and the pram gone. Again she looked up the road to see a different woman walking away with the pram.

"That's my baby!" screamed Mum pulling the pram away from her.

"She was crying so I thought I would take her for a walk." said abductor number two. Again Mum didn't know whether to believe her, but consequently she never left me outside again.

Mum and Dad decided to get a dog, a little dog of Heinz 57 variety. They called him Scamp and his name suited him down to the ground, because what a scamp he was! He used to open windows and get out. Mum and Dad couldn't keep him in. It was discovered that he had had distemper, and although he was cured of it, this disease left him slightly aggressive. So time went and on, and after getting out one day, he went for another dog that was being carried by a little girl. Unfortunately he missed the dog and bit the little girl, so sadly he had to be put down.

Dad was a printer. He had served a seven year apprenticeship. Now Dad had an ambition: he wanted to work on the big presses in Fleet Street, London. In order to get there, he had to gain a lot of experience in the trade, and so there began our wonderful journey.

CHAPTER 2

The start of that journey was when I was eighteen months old. We moved to Charlesfield Road, Rugby, Warwickshire, when Dad was offered his first step up the ladder.

Darren, the boy next door to us became my first pal. He was two, just six months older than me. Mary, his mum, and my mum became friends, so Darren and I would play together while they chatted.

One day Darren and I were playing outside. I was two and a half by then, and Darren was three. Most days we would either play in my garden or his, and that day Mum went next door and said to Mary, "Can you tell Glynis her dinner is ready, Mary?"

"What do you mean 'tell Glynis'?" replied Mary. "They're playing in your garden."

"No, they're in yours. Aren't they?"

Our mums gave each other a horrified look and promptly took off for the search, each in opposite directions. They met up outside the sweetshop at the end of the road. As they stood there wondering where to look next, a lady came out of the shop.

"Are you looking for your two little ones?" she asked.

"Yes," they replied in unison.

"They're playing on the swings down the road," she said. Mum and Mary fled down there quickly, shouting back behind them, "Thanks!"

On arriving there, Mum and Mary froze on the spot. There we both were, right at the top of the large slide, standing up having spotted Mum and Mary and waving frantically.

"Oo oo here we are! Look at us!" The two mums ran over to the slide and held out their arms to us, so we promptly slid down towards them.

"Don't you ever wander off by yourselves again. You gave us the fright of our lives," Mum said wagging her finger in the air at us. We never did it again.

I was quite an accident prone child, and still have a number of small scars that I acquired along the way. While living in Rugby, I was climbing up to the dining table one day, and I fell and cut the corner of my eye open. Now, Mum never was very good with blood back then so she immediately picked me up, ran next door, handed me over to Mary and then fainted, a ritual that was to be repeated many times in the future with various other people that were to hand. Another day I was out in the garden walking along the rockery when I slipped and cut my forehead open.

CHAPTER 3

In 1960 Dad wrote off for two jobs that he fancied and was offered both of them.

"Where do you fancy moving to? Southend in Essex or Letchworth in Hertfordshire?" he asked my mum.

"Oo lets go to Southend, it'll be nice to live by the sea," she replied.

So, we Puddles moved into Seaforth Grove, Southend on Sea. We had Mr and Mrs Waters further down to the left, living opposite us Mr and Mrs Pool, and a few doors to the right lived Mr and Mrs Flood. Well, what can I say? It doesn't get any wetter than that.

Dad worked on night shifts here so every week day Mum and I would walk to the end of the pier, which was one mile long, in order to leave the house quiet so my dad could get his sleep. We would take a flask of tea with us along with some biscuits and having consumed them would catch the train back, which ran backwards and forward along the pier. On returning home, if Dad wasn't up Mum and I would sit and knit or colour-in my colouring book.

Mum and dad decided to buy another dog, and Laddie, a first cross labrador/collie entered into our lives. Laddie was to become my trusted friend for a number of years to come.

I started school on my fifth birthday. Oh boy did I start with an outstanding performance. I promptly told the teacher in no uncertain terms that I didn't want to stay at school, and to make sure she understood, I kicked her in her shin. What a horrible child, you may all be thinking, but in my defence, I was starting to come down with the measles. Nobody knew it because there were no visual signs of it yet, but I was feeling rotten, and quite frankly couldn't be bothered with all this change in my lifestyle.

However, I settled down nicely in school once I was over the measles and as I started school in November, the highlight of my first year in school was about to come when it was time for the Christmas party. My grandad Saunders arrived for a visit with us and he came along to my school with my mum to witness this spectacular occasion, and I say 'spectacular' because it was. Father Christmas squeezed his large bulky frame down the chimney in our school hall, and delivered to all of us a wonderful present. I looked up at my grandad who was standing with my mum watching each of us receive our lovely gifts, and his eyes were glistening with tears; he was so moved by the proceedings.

I was invited to my first birthday party. Mum bought me an extremely pretty white party dress and I was so excited getting ready to go. Imagine Mum's surprise when we arrived on the doorstep and I handed over the present then announced.

"I'd like to go home now, please."

"But you haven't even got inside yet," Mum cried. I looked up at her with a pleading look.

"I'd still like to go home," I said. I had spotted all the children running around inside the house and suddenly felt a little nervous. So that was very nearly my first birthday party.

We acquired our first cat here, a kitten called Sandy. We got him from the family that invited me to the party. Sadly we didn't have him very long when Sandy stupidly took it upon himself to lie underneath a milk float that had arrived to deliver the street's milk. While the milkman was going about his deliveries, Sandy lazily fell asleep underneath the milk float and the milkman jumped into the driver's seat and promptly drove over him, quite oblivious to the fact that Sandy was lying underneath the float. I, of course, was heartbroken, so Mum asked the family if they had anymore cats. They did, and we acquired Sparky. He was black with white flecks that looked like sparks coming off him, hence his name.

I had made my second friend here in Southend, a little girl from Africa called Cindy. She was lovely and she got very upset when three years later I told her that we were moving away. Dad had written off for another job in Guildford in Surrey, and in 1963 we moved to an upstairs flat in York Road, Guildford. A Spanish lady lived in the bottom flat and all I can remember about her was a loud voice in a language I couldn't understand. She didn't mean to sound so loud and probably wasn't even aware of it, but the sound of this strange language was quite startling.

This wasn't to be the best move we ever made, however, as I became very ill with bronchitis. It seemed every time I left the flat I came down with it, so a pattern formed and I would be at school a fortnight and off sick a fortnight. This went on for the whole four months we lived there. The school had some concerns about me falling behind with my reading, so Mum was given some books for her to listen to me read, so I could keep up.

I had my sixth birthday in Guildford, but every Christmas was spent at Nana and Grandad's, and I slept in the back bedroom, which was later made into a bathroom.

Early one Christmas morning I woke up as the day was just beginning to break. I opened my eyes and very nearly jumped out of my skin. There was a figure in white standing at the foot of my bed. I sat bolt upright, rubbed my eyes and looked again. As my eyes became accustomed to the darkness, I realised the figure was a large doll, all dressed in white. She was simply beautiful. I called her Linda and she is still with me to this day. Nana and Grandad Saunders had bought her for me.

Later the following year, when I was six years old, I went on holiday to Bournemouth with Mum, Dad and Nana Puddle. We had a great time and Nana bought me a teddy bear. I called him Fred Frying Pan for some unknown reason and he is also still with me today.

One day Mum said, "I need to go to the shop and get a tin of peas."

"Can I go and get them?" I asked.

"No, you might get lost, love" said Mum. We hadn't lived there long at that time.

"No I won't. I know the way."

And I did, but it was raining that day and I had my hood up obscuring my vision. So when I came out of the shop having purchased the peas, I made a wrong turn, and having done so I didn't recognise where I was. As I searched for somewhere familiar I just got more and more lost. I stood on the pavement and cried. I was just thinking about what I should do, when a man in a red car pulled up beside me.

"Are you lost love?" the man asked. I just nodded. He got out of his car and came over to me.

"Can you tell me your address?" he asked me kindly, kneeling down beside me.

"Yes," I said and told him where I lived. Mum and Dad always made sure I knew my address at all times whenever we moved, so I was quite sure of that.

"Hop in my car and I'll drive you home," he said, smiling at me. Now, I absolutely knew I mustn't get into cars with strangers, but what was I supposed to do? The fact was I was lost and didn't have a clue how to get home. He saw me hesitate and immediately put me at ease. So I figured I had to take a chance. It was either that, or remain there.

"It's ok, I will take you straight home," he said sensing my apprehension. So I made a decision, got in and he drove me home. Mum was frantic when we arrived, but she thanked the man very much for his kindness. I was still holding the tin of peas.

I made a friend called Sarah, and one day some older girls that Sarah knew asked my mum if they could take me to the swings.

"Ok, but be careful and don't be too long," she said. As I was hanging over the swing face down swinging backwards and forward, I suddenly lost my balance and went head first onto the concrete ground splitting my head open in the process. The small swing area happened to be in a school playground and the caretaker, having seen the catastrophe came rushing over and I was bundled up to a room in the school. Huge plasters were placed over my head to stop the blood flow, and then I was taken home. On arriving home, imagine Mum's horror when she caught sight of my injuries.

"Oh no," was all she said. She was getting used to my frequent accidents.

Finally, one morning Mum came to get me up for school when she noticed my pillow had turned red and I had blood trickling from my mouth. The doctor was called out and Mum and Dad were advised to take me away from Guildford. He explained to them that Guildford was sitting in a valley and damp lingered there constantly. The fact was that this air just didn't agree with me. So it was time to leave another friend behind and continue on our travels.

CHAPTER 4

This is quite possibly one of the happiest chapters of my life. If you remember, Dad had been offered two jobs when we moved to Southend, the other one being in Letchworth. So Dad decided to reapply for that job and happily was offered the position once again. Wonderful.

So it was three weeks before Christmas, and I was wrapped up in a blanket, being ill once again. I travelled on my mum's lap in the front seat of our sidecar. With Laddie and Sparky sitting up in the back, we arrived in Caslon Way, Letchworth, Hertfordshire, in the afternoon. It was a very cold day, and a very kind neighbour popped round with cups of tea for everyone. Spotting me wrapped in my blanket, she said, "It's too cold for your little girl when she's not well. Bring her round to my house in the warm while the move is going on."

"Oh thank you," my mum replied, and off Mum and I went, round to the neighbour's cosy home.

I started my third infant school, and met my first best friend, Kate. Later we went on to start our first junior school together too. As luck would have it, we were put into the same class.

Kate and I shared a wonderful childhood over the next four years of being in Letchworth. I got well pretty quickly, and started

17

to eat properly again. I got stronger and stronger and put on loads of weight, going from a skinny little thing to being quite fat. What with my bright red hair and freckles, along with a load of fat around my middle I was not a pretty sight I can tell you, but I was extremely happy. I think it's fair to say, I had a quite perfect existence at that time of my life.

Ours was a modern house with a huge back garden, and although dad maintained the first half of the garden, which contained three apple trees, the back half was left wild and Kate and I would go on safari, making paths among the tall grass and plants. I was treated to a large swing system which contained an ordinary swing, a baby swing and a seesaw-type swing for two. I also had a wooden slide which I often got stuck on when it had been raining and was a little damp. Along with the large paddling pool which I acquired in Rugby, my garden was quite a kid's paradise.

On our front porch we had a large pole that Kate and I would dance and sing around. I could say Kate and I invented pole dancing, but I won't. However, someone really should have told me I couldn't sing, when I used to torture the neighbourhood with my version of Dusty's 'I Just Don't Know What To Do With Myself.' It astounds me that someone didn't tell me what to do with myself.

Every Friday on our way home from school, Kate and I would think up reasons why Kate should have a sleepover at our house for the weekend, so that we didn't have to separate at all. I don't know why we had to have a reason, because Mum and Dad and Kate's dad always said yes, but we felt we had to justify it. We pretended we were sisters, even though Kate had a little sister called Candy – we were so close we felt like family to each other. We shared many secrets and even had signs to each other to detect what each other was thinking. They were so secret I couldn't possibly divulge the contents.

We would play all sorts of games in the bright, warm atmosphere of the days: hopscotch; two ball; skipping. There was a craze of French skipping and all the girls were playing it, involving a long piece of elastic which would be stretched between two people's ankles. Then one person would skip in a sequence of steps, without getting tangled up. Gradually the elastic was raised until you did get tangled up. It was great fun. We would chalk out houses in the road and play neighbours. Sometimes, all the kids in the street would get together and we'd play 'What's The Time Mr Wolf?' where the person nominated as the wolf, would stand with their back to the rest and keep on turning around to shout out a time. When that person shouted 'Dinner Time' everyone else had to run, and the wolf would have to catch someone. Then it was their turn to be the wolf. We had lots of games like that and we all had a great deal of fun.

Kate and I were huge fans of The Monkees. My favourite was Davy Jones, and Kate's was Peter Tork. We even made up our own pop group, playing on pretend instruments and attempting to sing of course. We called ourselves 'The Elephants' which was quite appropriate really considering the loud and nowhere near pleasant noise we made. Saturday tea time was spent in front of the TV, while we watched The Monkees and Dr Who, and the rest of the evening we would play with our dolls. Our Sindy dolls played a big part in our lives.

Dad decided to trade our motorbike and sidecar in for a three wheeler Reliant car. One day Dad took a bend a little too near the kerb and the car hit it and tipped up. We were all ok but a little shaken up, so Dad went to the other end of the scale and traded it in for a Humber Super Snipe, a very superior car in my opinion. It had fold up picnic tables built in the back where I would play cards while travelling. Dad loved driving and we would go out for a picnic at the weekend, travelling for miles. The Humber had a bench seat at the front and I would sit on the arm between Mum and Dad. Seatbelts weren't around then. If Kate was with us, we would of course sit on the back seat playing games.

One day Dad was mowing the front garden lawn. I was playing

two ball against the house wall, and Laddie was tied on a long rope to the porch pole. Dad wandered across the road at one point to talk to a neighbour, and Sparky coming out of the side entrance, spotted Dad, and ran out into the road to go to him. Unfortunately there was a red car coming down the road. Of course Sparky hadn't seen it and there was a loud thud as it hit my beautiful little cat. Sparky was stunned, but got up and ran into our outhouse at the side of our house and buried himself at the back of it. Mum and Dad managed to eventually get him out, and rushed him to the vets. The vet did what he could but sadly the damage was too bad and Sparky died. Dad buried him in the back garden and Laddie would sit beside the tiny grave for hours. He must have missed him terribly, as we all did.

A few weeks later, I was sitting out on the kerb with my friend Evette who lived down the road on the opposite side (our mums were friends too), when Evette casually said, "We've just got a kitten."

"Have you?" I asked.

"Yes, d'you wanna come and see her?"

"Yeah."

So we went over to her house and there she was, a beautiful little tortoiseshell kitten. "Oh she's gorgeous. What's her name?" I asked.

"Suzy," said Evette.

Little did I know this pretty little cat was to become mine.

Now Evette had a little sister called Milly and it didn't take long before Milly became smothered in spots. Of course she was taken to the doctors by their mum and the doctor said, "It could be an allergy. Has anything changed in your household?"

"Well yes, we've got a cat. We haven't had her very long.

"Is there anyone who could look after the cat for a while, and we'll see if Milly's spots clear up?"

"Yes, my friend Margaret might look after her."

"That would be a solution," said the doctor.

So little Suzy was welcomed into our house, and pretty soon Milly's spots started to disappear. Hence it was a foregone conclusion that Suzy was here to stay. Laddie, of course took to her straight away.

What a wonderful cat. I loved her so much and she became my baby. I would dress her up in my doll's clothes, put her in my doll's pram and wheel her up and down the road. She looked so sweet, she was quite content to curl up in my pram and be taken out. I think it was the movement of the pram that made her fall asleep. She was quite oblivious to the fact that she looked ridiculous.

Now came the time when our everyday life changed slightly. I was seven and Mum decided to go back to work. She got herself a job working at our local Co-op supermarket and I was given a front door key. At first I kept on losing it, so Mum put it on a piece of string and I had to promise not to take it off from around my neck while at school, or playing out. There was usually an argument in PE lessons where I would promptly tell the teacher that there was no way I was taking this key from around my neck. My mum had told me not to take it off and that was that.

Mum had a very nice manager and during the school holidays Mum would take me along to work. On sunny days I would play out on the rough ground behind the shop with Neville, one of the other shop assistant's son. On rainy days I would sit in the manager's office colouring or reading. Sometimes he would help me colour-in my colouring book. I'm guessing he really should have been doing his own paper work but I suspect helping me was much more interesting. He was very kind and never made me feel in the way.

During term time Kate and I used to go down to our little row of shops on the estate, buy a bar of Bourneville chocolate at Fourboys or a 6d bag of chips at the fish and chip shop and go and play in the lift of the block of flats over the top of the shops. The caretaker of the flats would shout at us and chase us, waving his fist in the air. This was so much fun.

"This ain't a playground yer know. Clear orf!" he'd shout. But that just made the whole game of chase funnier. We'd charge around the passageways, running the poor man ragged.

I thought I would like to go to Sunday School. My nana was an avid Baptist church goer, and I decided to give it a try. I went to about four Sunday classes and then lost interest. After that I decided to go to Olde Tyme dancing classes, but if I'm honest it was the gold shoes we had to wear that attracted me, however I did last slightly longer than the Sunday School, but then I discovered Brownies. Kate and I started Brownies together. I was a Pixie, and every week I would get the Brasso out and proudly polish my badge just like dad had shown me, before putting on my brownie outfit. Kate and I enjoyed many evenings with Brown Owl and Tawny Owl.

After a time Mum decided to change her job and work in an office for a firm called ICL. While there she met a young girl called Avril. She was from Dublin, Ireland, and after observing her for a while Mum could see that Avril wasn't eating properly. She was living in a tiny bedsit which she could barely afford, and living on Marmite sandwiches. This girl clearly was not looking after herself so after consulting with Dad, Mum asked her over for a meal with us one night. I took to her straight away and so did Dad, so they asked her if she wanted to come and live with us so that Mum could make sure she ate properly. We had three bedrooms so it was no bother to us. Avril was delighted, and promptly packed her bags and arrived on our doorstep.

I spent many a happy hour with Avril. She would put makeup on my face and backcomb my hair, so I felt all grown up. She was like a big sister to me, and was wonderful company. But alas it wasn't to last, as one day her boyfriend Terry came and took her out into London for the day, which was where he lived, but not having much money they hitchhiked into London and back. Unfortunately they couldn't get a lift back so they ended up walking the whole way. It was a rainy night and two half drowned people arrived back at our house late that night. Of course my dad feeling responsible for this girl as she was living under our roof, launched quite a few chosen words at young Terry for walking Avril all that way in the pouring rain. Of course the very next day Avril announced that she was going to live in London with Terry, and we never saw her again. However she did send Mum and Dad a lovely letter thanking them for everything that they had done for her. She told them that while living with us, she had never been happier since leaving Dublin, but she loved Terry and wanted to be with him. So that was that.

A few weeks later a soldier in RAF uniform came knocking on our front door. He told us that he was Avril's brother from Ireland, and had been sent by their mother to check up on Avril as they hadn't heard from her for a while, and ours was the last address their mother had for her. Avril had told them all about us and they were pleased Avril was being looked after. However this family were about to be disappointed as Mum and Dad didn't have a forwarding address for her. We never did find out what happened to Avril and Terry after that; however Mum and Dad were invited to a rather posh RAF do by Avril's brother to which they happily went.

When I was nine years old, I was asked to be a bridesmaid for my mum's cousin, Joan, and her husband to be, Paul. I was dressed in a long, royal blue velvet dress trimmed with white Swansea fur, and carried a white prayer book in place of flowers. The wedding was lovely and at the reception when the best man stood up and announced a toast to the bride and groom, I hoped mine would have plenty of butter on it. As the minutes passed and there seemed to be no sign of any toast coming, I leaned over and whispered to Mum, "When's the toast coming?" Laughing, she explained that there was no actual toast, it was just a drink to wish the bride and groom happiness in their new life together.

"Well I wish they'd make it clear then." How disappointing, I thought.

Life was grand. I was still spending every waking moment with my best friend Kate. We were never apart, as we enjoyed day after day, lots of fun and laughter. However to quote a saying, 'All good things must come to an end.' Never a truer word has been said.

The dreaded day had arrived. I was ten years old and my world was about to cave in, as the horrific words were thrust upon my ears.

"We're moving to St Albans," Mum and Dad casually announced.

"NO!" I shouted. "I can't leave Kate!" I cried.

"Oh you'll make other friends," they said. Are they mad? Make other friends? Kate was the best friend a girl could have. I didn't want OTHER FRIENDS.

The day arrived only too fast, and as Kate and I hugged each other tight, tears rolling down our distraught faces. Of course we promised to keep in touch, but life was never going to be the same again.

CHAPTER 5

St Albans, a lovely old town. I say old because it is, and it is simply riddled with history. A wonderful place to live, and I soon began to amuse myself by exploring all the old buildings, walking around with my trustee friend, Laddie.

We hadn't lived there very long when Mum and Dad said, "How about Kate coming to stay with us for a few days, if it's ok with her dad?"

"Oooo yes please," I replied enthusiastically.

So off we went to Letchworth to fetch her back to our house where we spent a wonderful few days together. We went to the cinema to see 'The Wizard of Oz' and we walked up the clock tower which was my favourite place in St Albans. It has 311 steps, and when you get to the top, you can see all over St Albans. Quite wonderful. Kate was impressed. Later when my nana came to stay I took her up there too. It quite wore her out, poor Nana, but she managed to take it all in her stride. Both of my nanas were very fit for their ages and would attempt just about anything.

The house we lived in was very pretty, having ivy growing on the outside of it making it almost country cottage style. It had an attic which was allocated to me. Up there was my little sanctuary where all my favourite possessions lived, my blackboard and easel, my desk and chair, my Sindy, Patch, Suzy Cute and Fifi dolls and my dressing up clothes, among other things. There had been a family of ballroom dancers living in our road in Letchworth. They had won prizes for their dancing and possessed a number of absolutely stunning ballroom dresses, which they passed on to me for dressing up. I would parade around proudly swishing the magnificent material, in my element. My mum's wedding dress and some of her skirts were also among them for me to dress up in. A vivid imagination was apparent.

I didn't like going to school very much there. It wasn't so much the school, as the lack of friends. I was missing Kate and spent a lot of time on my own. I didn't mind being on my own of course, as I had a lot of toys to amuse me, and my dog Laddie and cat Suzy were my trusted friends. It wasn't long before it was the summer holidays, and I spent a long lazy summer just playing and exploring St Albans.

Mum and Dad both worked at the factory behind our house, and once the holidays arrived Mum and Dad were close enough to pop home for their breaks, where I would have a cup of Camp coffee and a cheese sandwich ready for them. Then they would be home around 17.00 and after tea we would spend the evening together in front of the TV. Sometimes Dad would work late and Mum and I would go up to the attic and wave to dad where he would be looking out of the factory window just before my bedtime.

One day Nana asked us if we would like her piano. "Can I learn to play it?" I asked when the beautiful piano arrived and I sat in front of it pressing the keys with one finger.

"Yes, if you want to," they said. So Mum booked some piano lessons for me.

My uncle Stan had come to visit us recently, informing us that his mother-in-law had died, whom he had lived with since his dear wife Auntie Gladys had passed away. He was actually my mum's uncle, my great uncle as he was my grandad's brother. We went over to Watford for the funeral and Uncle Stan took Mum and Dad to one side for a chat. I had no idea what the chat was about, and quite frankly I was more interested in his beautiful garden. It was huge, and had all sorts of things going on in it. There were prize dahlias, apple trees, all sorts of vegetables growing, a large shed, a lawn and a great big greenhouse right at the bottom. Beyond that was a piece of rough ground where Uncle Stan would burn all the garden waste. A winding path made its way right to the bottom. The garden was incredible.

At the end of the day we went home and I thought no more about it. That is until the Sunday before my first piano lesson was due.

"Come on, we're going to Watford to Uncle Stan's," said Mum.

Uncle Stan seemed very pleased to see us, but something wasn't right. There seemed to be a lot of whispering going on among them, until finally they sat me down and asked me if I liked the place. A little strange, I thought, after all we were only visiting.

"Yes, it's ok," I said warily.

"Well, Uncle Stan's asked us if we would move in with him, to look after him," said Mum.

"Oh, but I like it in St Albans," I said.

"Yes but it'll be nice living here in Watford with Uncle Stan. There's an airport at the end of the road; you'll be able to watch the aeroplanes taking off and landing," said Mum enthusiastically.

Yes, well admittedly that was quite interesting. I had never lived that close to an airport before, and to be honest we'd moved around so much that home to me was wherever I happened to be living at the time. I could adjust to anywhere. They showed me the sweet little bedroom I was going to occupy.

"Yes, it's nice. Are we going back to St Albans soon?" I asked.

"No, we're not going back. We're staying here. This is our home now."

"No! What about my piano lesson tomorrow?" I cried.

"Oh, don't worry. We'll get you piano lessons here," said Mum.

"What about all my dressing-up clothes and things?"

"It's ok, Dad's going back tomorrow to sort everything out," Mum reassured me.

Of course it occurred to me that they were going to struggle to fit everything in, what with Uncle Stan already having a house full of furniture, but I figured they knew what they were doing.

All of our belongings arrived at Ridgehurst Avenue in Watford but something was missing. Dad had forgotten to go up into the attic and all my favourite things had been left behind. He hadn't done it on purpose but I was heartbroken.

Uncle Stan also possessed a piano, so now we had two pianos in the house and still no sign of a piano lesson. Space was tight so Mum and Dad gave both the pianos away. I never did get my piano lesson but I thought no more about it.

Dad got a job at Odhams. This was a very large printing firm, he had now reached the top of his career, and I started my final junior school. Actually I fell lucky. They were about to arrange a school trip. A week in Swanage. Apart from staying at my nana's during the school holidays for the odd week this was to be my first separation from Mum and Dad. It went ok. I didn't feel at all uncomfortable, even though I hadn't really got to know anyone properly yet.

The time came to choose my senior school. I chose Francis Coombe because apart from the grammar school (if you were clever enough) and tech school, everyone else seemed to be going there. But alas, as the choosing of schools had already been started before I arrived in Watford, I couldn't get into Francis Coombe, and was told I was going to Leggatts School. When I was asked by fellow classmates which school I was going to, after telling them Leggatts, I have to say the reaction I got didn't exactly fill me with joy. It kind of went like this: "Oh no, you're not going THERE are you?" and "Sooner you than me, best of luck to you."

So when the morning arrived when it was time to head off in the direction of Leggatts School, to say I was a little nervous would be a huge understatement. To be quite frank I was petrified. Dad picked up on my apprehension and offered to walk me to the school on his way to work. He tried to reassure me.

"It won't be as bad as you think, love," he said. "You'll make some friends and you'll find everything will be ok. You'll come home tonight and wonder what you were worrying about." He smiled. When we got there, we stood in the playground where everything seemed a little daunting, and I looked around at everyone chatting and laughing. The teacher came over and Dad explained to her that I didn't know anyone.

"Oh we'll soon alter that," she said taking my hand. We waved Dad goodbye and she led me into the building.

I soon discovered that it really wasn't that bad. Dad was right, I soon made some friends and settled down to life at Leggatts School.

Living with Uncle Stan was absolutely wonderful. Every evening around 21.00, Uncle Stan would take Laddie out for a walk.

"D'you want to come with us?" he asked me one evening.

"Yes, ok," I quickly replied. So this became a ritual that I enjoyed every evening. Uncle Stan was nice to talk to and I would chatter away to him throughout our walk. I'm amazed he didn't get sick and tired of me wittering on, but he genuinely seemed interested in what I had to say. I loved his company and he seemed to like mine too.

Mum was beginning to get a bit bored staying at home all day so she got a job at Gade House, a huge departmental store in Watford High Street. She was employed in the women's Fashion department, but found the job a little tedious So after a while she got a job at Rolls Royce, which was based in the offices of the airport at the end of our road. She liked it there and remained there for all the time we lived in Watford.

I began to spend all my time with Uncle Stan. On Saturday mornings we would go along to the paper shop and Uncle Stan would buy me a comic and a quarter of chocolate limes. He would get his newspaper and tobacco and we would come home and sit in companionable silence, both engrossed in our reading material. Saturday afternoons would be spent in the garden with Uncle Stan gardening and me just playing.

Sundays were great. Uncle Stan used to tend to an old lady's garden in Sheepcot Lane. She was called Miss Green. That's it, Miss Green. I never knew her first name. She was always just Miss Green to me. Oh what a wonderful lady. She had lived in the same bungalow for all of her life. At first with her parents and brother, and then when her parents died and her brother was killed in the war she lived there alone, well apart from her two cats Patch and Parker. The woman was innocence at its very best, and I loved her. The three of us shared many a happy day.

Uncle Stan would work away in the garden, while Miss Green and I would sit and chat. We would all have tea and biscuits too. Butter Osborne biscuits to be exact. Life was truly wonderful. Miss Green was so funny. She had a number of very strange sayings, like: "You must eat your porridge, so's the wind doesn't whistle through your ribs." Also, she would tell my dog Laddie: "You should drink lots of water, 'cos lions drink water and look how strong they are." She had a saying for everything and was a constant delight to anyone who had the privilege to know her.

One day I arrived home to discover Laddie had been put to sleep. His kidneys had packed in and he was in a lot of pain. Dad had to make the heartbreaking decision to put an end to his suffering. Of course everyone was terribly upset. I cried my eyes out, and I could tell everyone else had shed a tear or two as well, despite trying to put a brave face on.

A couple of weeks later dad heard that there was a lady in Kings Langley who was selling rough collie puppies.

"Come on, we'll go and see them," Dad said cheerfully. I was so excited.

"Come on, Mum. Let's get going," I said heading for the front door. "Won't be long Uncle Stan. We're going to get a puppy," I informed him.

"That'll be nice." he said smiling.

We arrived at the house to find a beautiful rough collie mum and her six little balls of fluff scuttling around.

"You can have the pick of them," said the lady. As I stood there watching them all, one particular little puppy came over to me and just kept running around my feet. He looked up at me with the most melting eyes and I bent down and picked him up. As he nuzzled round my face, it was perfectly clear which one we were taking home.

"I think that one has picked you, love," said dad.

"Can we have this one?" I asked.

"Of course," said the lady. "But he's not quite old enough to leave his mum yet. You can pick him up in two weeks' time."

My heart sank. I wanted to take him home now. The lady saw my face.

"If you like, you can come and see him every day till he's ready."

"No," Dad said. "We won't bother you like that. We can see you've got your hands full here."

The two weeks soon went by, and it was finally time to go and collect my beautiful little puppy.

"What are we going to call him?" said Dad on the way home.

"How about Shep?" said Mum. Dad and I agreed that was a lovely name. I couldn't wait to show him to Uncle Stan. When we got home Uncle Stan was working in the garden. He looked up as we all walked down the garden path towards him. I had Shep in my arms.

"Hello, so this is the little fellow," he said, holding out his hand to stroke him. I was wearing a huge smile on my face.

"Isn't he gorgeous?" I said. "His name is Shep."

"Yes he's lovely," said Uncle Stan laughing at my beaming smile.

"I can't wait to take him out for walks with you, Uncle Stan."

"Well it won't be for a while," said dad, "cos he has to have all his injections first."

Now and again Dad would drive us back to Letchworth on a Friday evening. Mum and Dad would visit their friends, and I would call for Kate. One Friday evening in October after tea, Dad asked us if we fancied going through to Letchworth.

"Oo yes, I can tell Kate all about Shep," I said. After clearing the tea things away, the three of us got ready to set off.

"Look after my puppy, Uncle Stan," I called back as I skipped up the front garden path towards the car.

"Yes, I will," he said smiling.

As I waved goodbye to Uncle Stan, little did I know this was going to be, undoubtedly, the worst night of my life.

CHAPTER 6

It had been a lovely evening in Letchworth, and at around 22.00 we set off for home. Dad rented a garage a few streets away, so after dropping Mum and me off outside our house, he drove off to put the car away in the garage. Mum inserted the key into the lock and opened the front door. As we stepped into the hallway a peculiar smell reached our nostrils. Mum switched on the light and I noticed all of the internal doors leading off the hallway were shut. How unusual, I thought. They were always open as a rule. Mum was fiddling in her bag putting her key away.

"What's that funny smell?" I asked. Mum was smelling the air too.

"It smells like gas," she said.

I headed for the kitchen door and tried to prize it open. It seemed to be stuck for some reason. I gave it one almighty pull and it finally opened. Clumps of newspaper that had been jammed around the door frame fell to the floor. The kitchen light was on and I suddenly froze to the spot. My hand was still clutching the door handle as I stood staring at my uncle Stan, lying lifeless on the kitchen floor. He was holding the gas poker to his face. His bloodshot eyes were open and his skin was yellow from the gas. Without a doubt I knew my beloved uncle Stan was dead.

I said nothing, I couldn't move, and for a moment I couldn't hear anything either. Mum had come up behind me and she cried out when she saw him which made me jump. She quickly sprang into action, turning off the gas and opening the windows and back door. Still, I stood there just staring at him. Mum then went to the phone in the hall and dialled 999. Still, I stood there not moving. I knew that once I took my eyes off him I would never see him again, and I just couldn't bear that thought.

Mum started to prize the dining room door open next.

"Suzy's in here!" she said. "Shep must be in the front room."

She prised the final door open and out bounded little Shep. Mum put Suzy in the front room with Shep and shut the door again to keep them away from the gas. She went back into the dining room and everything fell silent. Eventually my mind returned to reality and I realised I was still clutching the kitchen door handle.

I wandered into the dining room to find Mum sitting at the dining table. She had a letter in her hand, and as she was reading it, the tears were rolling down her face. Why wasn't I crying, I asked myself.

"It's from Uncle Stan." She said in a strained voice. I didn't reply. I didn't seem to be able to speak. I had no idea why. Mum didn't embellish on the contents of the letter, but I guessed that it was Uncle Stan's explanation of his final actions.

Within a short time the house was full of police, firemen and ambulance men. At that point Dad arrived home. The front door was open and he just walked in. I could see the sheer disbelief and shock on his face. He spotted Uncle Stan on the floor and he looked at me, but I was still unable to speak and just pointed to the dining room where Mum was talking to the police.

The ambulance men put Uncle Stan onto a stretcher and covered him with a blanket. I could no longer see him and it felt final. I clung on to every last moment of him and watched as they carried him out, put him into the ambulance and slowly drove away. That was that. No more Saturdays and Sundays spent with him. No more long walks in the evenings. No more Uncle Stan.

I heard the fireman say to Mum and Dad, "You can't stay here tonight. Have you got somewhere you can go to? You have to stay away from this house for 24 hours to let the gas clear."

"Yes," said Dad "We can go to our parents' in Kent."

"Ok, good," said the fireman. "We've checked the house over and it's fine, just needs the gas to clear. You're lucky though, if anyone had come to the front door and rang the doorbell the whole house would have gone up."

The firemen left and Dad went to get the car back out of the garage again. We stood talking in the hallway to the policemen. One of them said to my mum, "This is clearly a suicide, I'll have to take this letter for evidence." Mum just nodded. "Make sure you lock the house up. I must insist you all leave now."

I picked up Shep, Mum picked up Suzy, we all stepped outside the front door and Mum locked up. I started to shiver in the cold night air. Dad was just pulling up in the car and Mum went round to the next door neighbours and knocked on their door. It was around midnight by now. The neighbours had been in bed but they came to the door, saw Mum's face and quickly ushered us all inside. After a tearful explanation of what had occurred, Mum asked them if they had seen or heard anything unusual coming from our house.

"No, nothing," they replied.

Eventually we all went into their lounge and sat down. A cup of tea was put into my hand.

"There, drink that, love. It's good for shock."

I wasn't sure who said it, and I still couldn't speak, but I took the cup and slowly sipped the hot tea. I kind of switched off and went into a world of my own while they were all talking, and after a while we left, got into the car, and set off for Nana and Grandad's in Kent.

"If we go straight to your mum's it'll still be too early. They won't be up for a while yet. We'll drive around London for a while, till it gets to a reasonable time," said dad.

He looked over his shoulder at me. "Settle down on the back seat love, and try to get some sleep," he said gently. Try to get some sleep, is he mad? But I lay down anyway and closed my eyes only to immediately open them again. It was no good; all I could see was my uncle Stan's body just lying on the kitchen floor. I sat up and looked out of the window trying to get the picture out of my head.

It was Friday night so London was alive with alcohol-fuelled people. We drove round Trafalgar Square and Piccadilly Circus and I watched the drunks prancing around making a lot of noise and showing off. Suddenly I wished I was them. Anybody but me right now.

We arrived outside Nana and Grandad's house at 05.30.

"I don't suppose they'll be up yet. We'll wait here for a while," said Dad. Nobody spoke after that and we sat there in silence with our own thoughts. At 06.00 the front room curtains twitched and then came flowing open. Nana was at the window. She hadn't noticed us parked outside. We all got out of the car and Mum knocked on the door. Nana opened it with a look of surprise on her face.

"What are you doing here at this time of the morning?" she asked.

"We've got some bad news, Mum."

"What is it?"

"Uncle Stan's committed suicide. We came home last night and found him dead," Mum said shakily.

Nana put her hands up to her face. "Oh no." She was very distressed. "I'd better get your dad up." Nana went up the stairs and I heard muttering coming from their bedroom. Nana came back down and Grandad followed a few minutes later.

"What happened?" His face was ashen. The shock of his brother's death was clearly visible.

"Sit down," said Nana gently. "I'll put the kettle on."

We all sat down and Nana brought the tea through. Mum and Dad related the events of the whole ordeal.

"We'll have to go and tell your uncle Bert," Grandad said to Mum. When everyone had finished their tea and Nana had taken the cups out into the kitchen, everyone got up ready to set off for the third brother's house to break the terrible news. I got up too.

"No love, you stay here. Uncle Bert will be very upset. You'll be better off staying here in the warm. Why don't you read your book or do some colouring. You can sit in Grandad's chair. We won't be long.

They all left and the house fell silent. I stood there for a moment, not quite knowing what to do. I went over to grandad's chair and sat down. I began to feel uneasy. The feeling grew stronger and stronger. I couldn't understand it. I'd been left on my own many times before, this was no big deal. What on earth was the matter with me. Suddenly the old clock on the sideboard struck the hour and it made me jump. It was 10.00 and the chimes seemed to be getting louder and LOUDER. WHAT WAS HAPPENING? My heart was pounding. I became very frightened. OF WHAT? I DIDN'T KNOW. I had to get out of there. I got up and ran down the hallway. The panic I felt was tremendous. I yanked the front door open and ran into the cool October air outside. I was shaking and I felt hot and clammy.

It was only a small front garden, a forecourt really with a hydrangea plant in front of the window. I left the door open so as Shep could follow me out and thankfully he did, because there was no way I was going back inside. I stood with my back to the gate watching Shep sniff around the little garden. Suzy was ok, she was asleep upstairs on Nana's bed. She always slept after a car journey. I have no idea how long I was stood there, but eventually everyone came back with solemn faces.

"What on earth are you doing out here in the cold?" said Mum.

I couldn't very well say I was frightened, that would sound ridiculous, so I made out Shep had wanted to go out, and they seemed to accept that.

Later we went to my other grandparents flat briefly, to tell them what had happened. It was too soon to return to Watford, so we stayed the night at Nana's house. The next day was Sunday and it was time to go home. We travelled in silence, contemplating the thought of going back to the vision of what had happened. At least I know I was.

As I walked through the door, I shuddered at the thought of the discovery of the last time I had come home. I stared at the kitchen floor where Uncle Stan had spent the last moments of his life, and an unbelievable sadness overwhelmed me. Mum and Dad were bustling around, and without thinking about what I was doing, I strangely found myself following them around from room to room. I couldn't seem to bring myself to be alone. This was ludicrous but I couldn't help it. I tried to go upstairs to my room, but I got halfway up the stairs and my heart started to pound. I started to panic and shake. I ran back down to the front room where Mum and Dad were.

"I thought you were going up to your room, love," said Mum.

"No, I don't think I'll bother," I said casually, and sat down with them. I tried to hide my fear. I don't think they noticed. Then I started to worry. What on earth was I going to do at bedtime? At Nana's I had slept on a camp bed in Mum and Dad's room as it was only a two bedroom house now that the smallest bedroom had been made into a bathroom, but here, obviously I would be expected to sleep in my own little room.

Night time arrived and I followed Mum upstairs when she went to get ready for bed, but when she went downstairs, I followed her.

"Aren't you going up to bed now, love? You have school in the morning." It had just been half term so I'd been off all last week.

"No, I think I'll stay up for a while." I said.

I could see Mum and Dad glance at each other. This wasn't like me, I normally went up to bed quite early. I liked to go and read for a while. They knew something was wrong.

"D'you wanna sleep in our room tonight, love?" said Dad.

"Yes, ok," I said casually. But we all knew this was never done. I loved my own room, and was happy with my own company usually. Mum and Dad always stayed up late, so around midnight we went up together. Straight away I got into the middle of the bed in order to feel safe. Dad passed me a book.

"Have a read of this for a while," he said. When the light was turned out, I felt a knot in my stomach, but it wasn't panic-stricken because I could hear Mum and Dad's gentle breathing. Eventually I fell asleep.

The next day I went to school. In the English lesson, we were asked to write about what we did in the half term holiday. I hadn't said anything to anyone about what had happened, but in my essay it all poured out. I wrote down exactly what had happened and casually handed it into my teacher. The next English lesson, my teacher stood at the front of the class with the pile of our books beside her. She slid the top one off and opened it.

"I would like to read one of your essays out to the class. This piece was very moving and I would like you all to share it. That is with your permission, Glynis?" she added looking straight at me. OH NO, it's mine. I want the floor to open up I thought. But I slowly nodded to her, and she read it out. How could she do this? What am I going to do? I couldn't move, so I just sat there speechless. When she had finished reading, the room was silent, and my teacher merely said, "Not everyone had a good half term holiday."

Life went on, but my fear would not subside. I couldn't even bring myself to go into the house on my own after school. Instead, I would stand in the front garden for an hour or so, rain or shine, until Mum or Dad arrived home, after which would follow the same ritual of following them around the house and sleeping between them at night. I wasn't used to staying up late but I would fall asleep on the sofa and Dad would carry me up at bedtime.

CHAPTER 7

One Saturday morning Mum and Dad announced that they had to go somewhere. It was to do with Uncle Stan's estate and I wasn't allowed to go.

"You'll be ok here," they said. "Find something to occupy yourself. You'll be fine."

"Can't I come with you and wait in the car?" I pleaded.

"No, love," they both said. They saw my face and Dad sat me down.

"Look, love. What you have to remember is that Uncle Stan loved you very much, he would never hurt you, ever, so you mustn't be frightened of him now he's dead."

I nodded, but I wasn't convinced. But I realised it was awkward for Mum and Dad, and that sometimes I must stay on my own. I mean, this was silly. I'd stayed on my own many times before all this happened, if only this fear would go away.

I stood in the hallway and watched as they closed the front door behind them. It was a glass panelled door and as I stood there, two figures appeared on the front step and rang the doorbell. I felt so relieved, I didn't care who it was, as it meant even if only for a minute I wasn't alone, so I opened the door. Two men were standing there. One had a very large camera, the other one held a notebook and pencil.

"Hello darlin'," the one with the notebook and pencil said cheerfully.

"My mum and dad are out!" I said.

"It's ok, how about we talk to you?" he asked. Clearly they'd been waiting for Mum and Dad to leave before they knocked, but I didn't realise that at the time. I toyed with my thoughts. I knew I definitely should not let strangers into the house. That instruction had been drummed into me at an early age, so I wasn't in any doubt as to what I SHOULD do, but then on the other hand there was my fear of being alone. Unfortunately the latter won, and I opened the door wider for them to enter the house. This, of course, was going to be a huge mistake.

The one with the notebook was extremely chatty. He kept on complimenting me on how I looked, this was weird and had never happened to me before, and after all I was only twelve. He started asking me about my uncle Stan.

"I expect you miss him a lot don't you?"

"Yes, I do. Why? Did you know him?" I replied

"No, but I know he must have loved you a lot to leave you all that money." I didn't reply. I just looked at him suspiciously. He seemed to pick up my thoughts so he quickly changed his tactic.

"How would you like your photograph in the newspaper like a film star? Would you like that?" He smiled at me.

"Ok," I shrugged. The other man with the camera hadn't said anything up until that point but he suddenly sprang into action.

"Perhaps you can sit on the stairs, maybe with your dog," he said lifting the camera up ready to take a photo. I took hold of Shep's collar and led him up the stairs.

"That's it," he said "Just about there will be great." I sat down and pulled Shep down beside me. There were a lot of flashes from the camera while he took his shots.

"Oh you're like a model," he said, encouraging me to smile at him.

Give them their due, they were extremely good at what they did, and that was to get a story for their newspaper. I have to say I was enjoying the attention these two happy chappies were giving me.

Suddenly the front door opened and Mum and Dad walked in.

"WHAT THE!!!!" my dad shouted. "WHO THE HELL ARE YOU?"

"Hello, Sir, we are from the *Evening Echo,*" the writing one said.

"GET OUT!" dad shouted, and he pushed them both out of the door. Then he turned to me. "WHAT ON EARTH DO YOU THINK YOU ARE DOING LETTING STRANGERS IN? YOU KNOW BETTER THAN THAT." I'd never seen him so angry.

"They took photos of me. I'm gonna be in the newspaper," I stated in my defence. Dad just shook his head. He knew at that point, the trouble that was about to occur.

"Glynis, this is my trade. I know the damage these blokes can cause," he said sighing. "You've made a huge mistake here!"

What's the worst that can happen, I thought. I couldn't help thinking dad was overreacting. But he wasn't. The newspaper popped through the letterbox that evening, and there I was, front page headlines:

GLYNIS, AGED 12, IS LEFT £2,000

A large photograph of me and Shep accompanied the story. I was thrilled. I ran into the front room waving the newspaper in the air.

"Look, I'm on the front page," I said excitedly. I handed it to Dad and he took one look at it and shook his head.

"Oh no," he simply said. I was quite disappointed in his reaction. I expected far more enthusiasm than that.

"What d'you think of the photo?" I prompted.

"The photo's great, it's the consequences that worry me," he replied, handing the newspaper to Mum. She didn't say anything, she just read the article and gave the newspaper back to Dad.

Well, that was disappointing, I thought.

Monday morning arrived, and I set off for school. Everyone crowded around me questioning me, wanting to know all about Uncle Stan and his desperate final actions, but I really didn't want to talk about that and so I just stood there in a daze. Other kids passing shouted various comments out to me, like: "Watchya, little rich girl" and "Give us a loan!"

Two thousand pounds was a lot of money back then, you could buy a house outright with that amount. To be honest I hadn't really thought about the actual money. I was more interested in the fact that I was on the front page of the newspaper.

I had a wonderful day at school. I was the centre of attention and I loved it. What I didn't realise was, that times were going to get bad. Really bad.

After school a couple of days later, I set off for home. I got down the road and there were three girls standing by the bus shelter. As I approached them they blocked my path so I had to stop.

"Give us some money then," one girl demanded.

"Yeah, all of us," another one sneered.

My heart began to pound again. "I haven't got any money," I said in a meek voice.

"Leave it out, we saw you in the paper," the third girl shouted in my face, and with that she pushed me.

I stumbled backwards and just looked at them.

"If you'd read the article properly you'd know I can't have that money till I'm twenty-one." I tried to sound arrogant, but somehow I just sounded desperate.

They realised that they were not going to get any money, so they hit me, all three of them, and I fell over. They started kicking me, and I curled up in a ball trying to protect my head. Someone across the road shouted at them and they ran off. I got up, brushed myself down and looked over to where the voice had come from, but my saviour had gone.

I limped home, feeling sick and sore. I wanted so much to go indoors and recuperate. I put my key in the lock and started to open the front door. Shep ran out to me, but the familiar panic took hold of me and I quickly shut the door again. I wanted to sit down, but there was nowhere to sit, only the front doorstep, and I couldn't sit there because my back would be to the door, that thought just made me panic again. So I stood as usual, by the gate. Shep ran around the garden busying himself with all the different smells he could find, and I watched him until I saw Mum coming down the road. I opened the gate for her.

"Ok?" she asked.

"Yes," I replied.

I always tried to hide the fact that I couldn't go into the house because I felt stupid, making up different excuses as to why I was in the front garden.

"I thought Shep wanted a wee," I said. Mum just smiled.

A couple of days later, a different group of girls confronted me in a similar manner, ultimately after the same thing. Money. Again I eventually escaped and ran home to lick my wounds. I began to realise what my dad had meant when he said he knew the damage those reporters could cause. If I hadn't been in the newspaper these girls wouldn't be bullying me. At that point I wished Uncle Stan hadn't left me that money.

Day after day I had to endure this same horrendous treatment from various girls – I just couldn't get away from them. I didn't understand why they kept on at me once I'd told them I didn't have the money. Why couldn't they just leave me alone. I DON'T HAVE ANY MONEY.

Pretty soon I didn't know which way to turn. I was scared to go to school for fear of getting beaten up, but I was also scared of the house. I would crouch in a corner whenever I found myself alone. The atmosphere would spin and I would shake. I was having a breakdown, although I didn't realise it myself. Mum and Dad did their best but I hid the contents of my mind, and the cuts and bruises on my body, so well that they didn't know the half of it.

Then one day Mum caught me checking out a lump on my head in the mirror.

"How did you get that?" she asked sifting through my hair to reveal the huge lump.

I finally broke down right in front of her. Everything that had been going on suddenly came gushing out. She hugged me and told me that they would sort it out.

"Everything will be fine," she said.

Mum and Dad went to the school shortly after that to speak to the headmaster.

"Is it possible for you to arrange for someone to collect her from school each day?" the headmaster asked.

"No," said Mum. "We both work, and there isn't anyone else."

"You see, we can keep an eye on her here, but once she leaves the school we can't do anything," he said sadly. "The only other thing I can suggest is that I may be able to get a member of staff to escort her home." Mum and Dad agreed: that would be acceptable.

Later, Mum and Dad sat me down. "Now look, a teacher called Mr Tomms is going to escort you home each day. You must go and find him when you finish your last lesson. He'll be in the science huts."

"Ok." I said.

I felt a little happier about going to school, but not much. They would sometimes start on me during dinnertimes and breaktimes as well, but I'd worked out a while ago now, that as long as I stayed away from the toilets where they seemed to congregate, and placed myself as near to any teachers as I could, I would stay fairly safe. But from then on I would drift off during lessons where my thoughts were constantly planning my moves, so as not to leave myself alone or vulnerable. For a while, it was fine; I would go and find Mr Tomms as soon as the end of school bell rang, and he would drive me home. Sometimes I would see girls hanging around as we drove down the road. My stomach would churn, but at least I was safe. Mr Tomms would drop me off outside my house and I would wait in my front garden as usual, till Mum and Dad came home.

One day it was pouring with rain while I was waiting in the garden, when Mrs Jackson, the elderly lady next door came out.

"What are you doing standing in the rain, dear?" she asked kindly.

"I forgot my key," I lied.

"Oh dear, well come in here with us till your Mum and Dad get home." I was grateful for the offer and went round to meet her. "Come on dear, take your wet coat off and I'll make some tea," she said, as I stepped into her kitchen.

The kitchen was old fashioned but very cosy and it smelt of baking. The heat from the oven instantly made me feel warmer and my shivering subsided.

"Don't stand on ceremony," she smiled. "Go through to the living room and sit down. I'll just make the tea."

I went through to see Mr Jackson sitting in his armchair by the fire. He was reading his newspaper and he put it down as I came in.

"Hello, love. What's all this then, you standing out there in the rain?"

"I forgot my key," I lied again.

Mrs Jackson came in carrying a tray, containing three teacups of hot tea and a plate of freshly baked rock cakes. They gave each other a look and I got the feeling they'd seen me out there before, but they didn't say anything so I just sat down on their old fashioned sofa and Mrs Jackson handed me a cup of tea.

"Would you like a rock cake?" she asked, holding the plate in front of me.

"Thank you," I said taking one from the plate. We made small talk for about an hour, then Mrs Jackson got up from her chair.

"I'll just go next door and see if your Mum or Dad's home yet dear."

"Ok."

I was enjoying the peaceful atmosphere in this quite pretty room, with all its floral and many ornaments and pictures.

A few minutes later Mrs Jackson returned with Mum in tow.

"Come on, let's get you home," said Mum. I expected her to say something about me forgetting my key again, but she didn't.

Later, while sitting watching TV, Dad casually said, "What's this about you forgetting your key again love? You never used to keep on forgetting it like this."

I just shrugged and continued to stare at the TV. I didn't even see what was on the screen, I was just racking my brains to think of an excuse for my behaviour. I couldn't say I was still scared, that would sound ridiculous. I could see Dad was trying to address this delicately, but I was hoping he would drop the subject because I couldn't think of a single thing to say.

"You're not still worried about Uncle Stan are you? 'Cos I've told you before there's nothing to be scared of in this house."

"I know," I said without looking up. I was sitting in the swivel chair to our three piece suite. You could make it rock too, although you wasn't supposed to, but I was now rocking the chair frantically. Dad, sensing that I was uncomfortable with this line of questioning, left it there.

Gradually Mr Tomms lost interest in taking me home. You couldn't blame him – it must have been a bit of a nuisance having to drive me home every day. After all, it was extremely good of him to do it until now. So when I couldn't find him, I would hide somewhere in the school grounds until I was sure everyone had gone, and I felt it was safe to walk down the road. I really wished I was tougher and able to put up a decent fight. But there were always a few of them so I really didn't stand a chance. That's the thing with bullies, they never bully alone.

It was sports day at school. I was standing at the edge of the field watching the events. I had done my bit, the long jump, bad as I was at it, at least I participated. Well that was my view anyway.

Actually it was quite an understatement to say I was bad at sports, I think it's fair to say I was downright useless. Whether it was netball, tennis or hockey, whenever any sized ball came my way during lessons, you can be sure I would not be paying the slightest bit of attention to it. I would constantly be getting shouted at by the PE teacher.

"Glynis! Pay attention, will you?"

"What? Oh my gawd, have I missed it again?"

While I was standing there, one of the girls in my year came over to me. She was unpopular too, although for a different reason. She was picked on because of her scruffy appearance. It wasn't her fault, she came from a large family who couldn't afford a lot, but kids could be cruel, as I well knew.

"Oi, Glynis. You meet me in the car park, 'cos I'm gonna kick your 'ead in." I gave her a puzzled look.

"What?"

"You 'eard." She sneered at me, and with that she sprinted off the field.

I didn't get it, she was as unpopular as me. Why on earth would she turn on me like that? I looked over to where she was heading and spotted a bunch of bullies standing a distance away laughing. What was the matter with her? Couldn't she see that they were just using her to get their kicks, and at my expense? I began to feel angry at this girl for turning on me and pandering to their nonsense. Even so, my stomach was doing its usual somersaulting.

I went to the changing rooms when the events were over and we were allowed to go home, got changed and set off for the inevitable. As I walked down the road I could see a crowd of the usual bullying bozos and her, standing with her arms folded and a smug look on her face. Who the hell does she think she is, I thought. At that point something snapped inside me. I dropped my bag on the ground, ran up to her and grabbed her by the hair. I have absolutely no idea where my strength came from, but I literally rammed her face straight down into the stony gravel of the car park. Time and time again her face hit the gravel and then she started screaming. The scream startled me and I let go of her hair. She lifted her face up and I could see all the tiny stones embedded into her face. I don't know who was more shocked, her, me, or the bullies, but the gruesome crowd started cheering, and she ran off down the road. I just stood there feeling sick at what I had done. The crowd dispersed and I found myself standing alone, but unharmed for once. I picked up my bag and slowly walked home in a daze. How could I do something like that? But it was her or me, I told myself, desperately trying to justify my actions. That kind of behaviour was definitely not my nature. Later, I told Mum and Dad what I had done.

"Well, it sounds as though she asked for that, love," said dad. "Serves her right for trying to impress those hooligans." Dad always knew what to say to make me feel better.

After that, the bullies kind of left me alone. I got the odd taunt during school time, but there was no one waiting for me after school anymore, no more cuts or bruises.

I made friends with a couple of boys in my class, Ivan and Peter. They weren't part of the 'in crowd' either and the three of us didn't like PE or games, so on PE days we would meet up by the bike sheds, which were situated by the school gate. The headmaster's office overlooked this part so we had to be very careful not to be seen. Ivan and I would crouch down by the bike shed and Peter would go ahead and signal for us to run out of the gate. The three of us would then either go up to Chilcott and get some chips on the way to the park, or we would head back to my house and I would make jam sandwiches for us. We would sit around listening to records and chatting. They both came from large families and they enjoyed the peacefulness of my house.

Over a time Dad had changed the whole appearance of the house room by room. Everything was different in order to erase the bad memories of that terrible night. Central heating was installed and new carpets were put down. Dad decorated throughout. The whole house became modern and new. Mum and Dad moved into Uncle Stan's room and I got their old room. The little bedroom was now spare. I had turned fourteen by now and Mum and Dad asked me if I would like a nice modern teenage bedroom.

"We'll do it all out nice and you can choose the wallpaper. You can have whatever colour you want," said Mum.

"Yes," I said.

I suppose I'll have to go back into my room at some point, I thought, but I wasn't sure how I would deal with it yet. Dad built fitted wardrobes across one wall from floor to ceiling in teak wood with one door mirror tiled and a small dressing table built in. His mate from work helped him as he had done this before. Mum and I picked out wallpaper, carpets and curtains. They gave me a coffee table instead of a bedside table on which a stylish lamp and a radio were placed. The colour scheme was orange, very modern in the early seventies. When it was finished I was thrilled. I put all my posters of my favourite pop stars on the walls: Elvis Presley, David Essex, The Osmonds and the Bay City Rollers were my favourite at the time although there were many others I liked too.

It was time to face the night in my own room. Perfect as it was, there were still some demons lurking, as I discovered when Mum and Dad went to shut my bedroom door on the first night. At first I tried to stall them, by pointing out all the lovely things in my room.

"Yes, we know," they laughed. "Settle down and read your book," said Mum.

"D'you want your radio on?" asked dad.

"Ok."

He put the radio on and tuned it into Capitol Radio, a local London radio station. As soon as the door shut I sat staring at it. I had this feeling it would open and something or someone was going to come in and kill me. An illogical assumption I know, but nevertheless to me it felt real. No, it was no good I didn't feel safe. I HAD TO FEEL SAFE. I opened the door.

"What's the matter?" said Dad. I felt silly then.

"Nothing," I replied. But Dad knew there was.

"Look, would you feel better if you could lock the door?" he asked.

I nodded. The doors were solid and old fashioned and there was a lock and key on each one. Dad pointed to the lock.

"Just turn the key, love. It might make you feel better. But there's absolutely nothing to fear," he added, looking at me with concern.

I closed the door again and turned the key. Yes, that felt a bit better. I got into bed, read for a while and then turned out the light. No, it was no good, the darkness was frightening. I switched the light back on. I sat up and watched the lock. It's ok, the key was not turning. I was safe I told myself. As long as I could see the key I didn't panic, so I continued to watch it until I eventually fell asleep. This same ritual was maintained every night. It had been almost two years since Uncle Stan had gone: why couldn't I think normally again?

CHAPTER 8

Eventually the fear did subside and I began to sleep soundly without the silly ritual every night. I began to make some more friends at school and one girl in particular became my best friend. Her name was Verity, and we started going to the airport clubhouse and various other places. Dad said I could go as long as he picked us up at the end of the night; he didn't like the idea of us coming home on our own. We didn't drink any alcohol, we were content with orange juice and having a dance round our handbags. As you do.

One day Verity and I were out with a few friends in the woods next to our school, when a boy who I didn't know joined us. He was from a different school. He was a tough kind of boy, you could tell by his appearance. He wore a black Crombie and loafers and had shoulder length, blond curly hair. And oh! But he was gorgeous. We were all walking along casually, when he took my hand and gently pulled me to one side.

"I've been told you ain't got a boyfriend," he stated. I just shook my head. "Can I be your boyfriend then?" he asked.

"Dunno," I shrugged. He took my other hand and swung my arms backwards and forward.

"I won't bite," he smiled.

"Alright then." I smiled back nervously.

So this was it, my first boyfriend.

"What's yer name?" I asked him.

"Terry Patterson," he replied confidently. "I know yours."

We walked hand in hand and caught up with the others.

"I'm not sure of him," I said to Verity later.

"Well, if you don't want to go out with him, tell him you don't want to," she said logically.

I did want to go out with him, who wouldn't. He was gorgeous, but if I was honest I was just a bit nervous of him. He was clearly a tough guy.

"Why don't you go out with him once, and if you don't want to go out with him again, you don't have to." Verity was much wiser about boyfriends than I was as she already had a boyfriend. It was no big deal to her.

"Ok, I will," I said decisively.

"Would you be happier if Colin and I went along with you?"

"Oh would you? That would be great."

Later that evening our phone rang. I was upstairs in my bedroom. Mum answered it.

"Glynis, it's for you," she shouted up the stairs. I ran down and took the phone off her.

"Thanks," I said. "Hello?"

"Watchya, it's Terry. I've got to babysit round at my sister's tomorra night. Fancy coming along to keep me company?"

"Ok, d'you mind if Verity and Colin come too?"

"Why not, we'll 'ave a laugh." He told me the address, and said to come round about seven o'clock.

Dad wasn't sure about him. He thought Terry should call for me so as they could meet him.

The following evening the three of us set off for Terry's sister's house. The evening went brilliantly. We played records by T Rex, David Bowie and a few others. We had a good laugh and didn't hear a peep from the children upstairs. I felt great. If this was

53

dating, I could certainly get used to it.

At school, about six weeks later, a couple of the 'in crowd' girls came up to me.

"Is it true you're going out with Terry Patterson?"

"Yeah," I said suspiciously.

"My God, what on earth does he see in you?" they sneered, and then they walked away giggling together.

A couple of weeks later Terry phoned me up.

"Look, sorry but I don't want to go out with you anymore," he said.

"Ok." I didn't know what else to say. I was devastated. My voice was shaky.

"I'll see you around," he said.

"Yeah."

I put the receiver down, ran upstairs and flung myself on the bed. I was crying my eyes out when Mum appeared at the door.

"What's the matter, love?"

"He chucked me," I sobbed. She came over and put her arms around me.

"I'm sorry love."

She just hugged me for a while. There wasn't a lot she could say. I was inconsolable. She finally got up to leave.

"Never mind there's plenty of fish in the sea, love," She added lightly. But who wants to go out with a fish, I thought grumpily.

"Well, he was no good anyway," Dad said later. Dad had joined the special constabulary at Watford police station, and he seemed to have a knack of being able to sum people up. He had only met Terry once during the short romance but it was enough for him to have figured Terry out. He tried to convince me I was better off without him, and he too mentioned the fish thing. What was it about fish and breaking up?

I was still going to visit Miss Green every Sunday. I would talk everything through with her over tea and Butter Osborne biscuits.

"Well I think your dad's right," she confirmed. "I don't think he was right for you."

I only ever missed seeing Miss Green for one Sunday in every two months, as we would get together with Mum and Dad's friends – Jane and Rob with their son Ken, who was two years older than me. They used to live opposite us when we lived in Letchworth. One month they would visit us and the next we would visit them. When they came to us I still had time to visit Miss Green as they didn't arrive until around 11.30.

I looked forward to this monthly get-together. Ken and I were great friends; we still are to this day. After all, we grew up together. We were never bored with each other's company. We would listen to music. He liked Simon and Garfunkel. Ken was a brilliant artist and he would try to teach me but it seemed he was fighting a losing battle there as I couldn't draw to save my life. Sometimes in the summer we would go out and pick flowers, some of which came from people's gardens I'm ashamed to say, and we would bring them back, put them in a bucket of water and stir. We loosely called it perfume. It never turned out right for some reason, but it was fun to do. Once Ken poured vinegar into the end product and it smelt horrible. I found that hilarious. Ken always knew how to entertain me.

Life at school was much better now. Verity and I had a few lessons together, one of them being 'Environmental Studies'; it wasn't a CSE subject so it was pretty relaxed. Admittedly we made it slightly more relaxing than it should have been, but that was beside the point. While we were supposed to be going round places of work collecting information, what we were actually doing was either going to one of our houses, if there was an Elvis Presley film on TV to watch, or getting on the Underground and going up to Oxford Street to look around the shops. We would sit on the train for ages doing what we called 'people watching'. We would have a great time trying to guess where people were going, what they did for a living... etc. We stupidly thought our skiving went unnoticed, until one day our headmaster stopped us in the corridor, as we were just leaving to go on our project.

"Hey! You two. Where're you going?"

"We're going up to the Ideal Home Exhibition, to collect leaflets on the latest technology, Sir."

"Ok then, but while you're in Oxford Street, do me a favour and get me a birthday card for my wife will you? I'm no good at choosing the right card." He smiled. "Here's some money." He handed us a pound note. "Thanks, I want change though."

"Ok," we both replied happily, and we hurried away.

The next day, we went to find our headmaster to give him the card we'd taken great care in choosing, and his change. Two days later we saw him in the corridor again.

"Just a moment, you two. I have to say, you made too good a job in choosing that card you know. My wife didn't believe I'd chosen it." He laughed, and he walked away.

We stood looking at each other, puzzled.

"So, did we do right or wrong?" I asked Verity.

"I'm not sure," she said slowly as she shook her head.

Around this time, my nana received a visit from a couple from up near the Lake District, a place called Barrow-in-Furness. They said they were distant relatives of ours and were down in Kent to seek us out. They told Nana and Grandad that there were quite a few other relatives up there too. When Nana and Grandad told Mum and Dad about the visit afterwards, they decided that we should all travel up to Barrow-in-Furness for a holiday in order to meet them all.

What a wonderful holiday we had! A few of the relatives owned caravans or huts in a big field down on the coast road, and everyone would congregate there.

"No need to go round visiting everyone, they all come here at some time or another," said Auntie Ellen.

It was true, they did. It was so relaxing there and they all made us very welcome, and genuinely seemed pleased to meet us. I would wander along the beach with Shep. It was lovely, far from the hustle and bustle of our London streets. We returned home feeling very relaxed and we promised we would visit again.

We did return the following year in the autumn. My cousin Juliette from Newcastle came to stay with us in Watford for ten weeks. We introduced her to the sights of London, and to finish off her holiday, Mum and Dad took us back to Barrow-in-Furness. As it was autumn, all the relatives down at the coast road had returned to their houses for the winter, so we were very kindly lent one of the caravans for a week. It was quite bleak there at that time of year, but still wonderful. Juliette really enjoyed it too. The caravan was nicely kitted out and we were very cosy. We were all becoming very attached to Barrow-in-Furness.

I had discovered an old sewing machine in the house which had belonged to Uncle Stan's wife, and I started making my own clothes. Mum would often come home from work to find me wearing one of her sheets as my latest creation. Of course while Juliette was here two sheets would go missing and Mum would find us parading around in pink smocks when she got home. After the holiday it was time to say a sad farewell to Juliette and take her home to Newcastle. She was great company and I desperately wanted her to stay forever.

"Auntie Sheila and Uncle Eric will want their daughter back, love," said Mum. "As much as we'd like her to stay, Saffron and Pricilla also want their sister back. She can come again though, if she wants to."

We kept in touch with Dad's sister, Auntie Sheila, and Uncle Eric with regular trips up to Newcastle, so it wouldn't be long before we would see them again. I pacified myself with that thought. Growing up, my cousins and I would have joking disagreements as to who spoke correctly. They said that they had the proper accent, Geordie, but I told them no, I spoke the Queen's English. Well kind of.

Verity and I were almost fifteen when we decided to go to night school to learn shorthand and typing. We had a typing lesson once a week at school, but shorthand wasn't taught there at all. So twice a week we would get on the bus outside our school and go to Casio college. We would have our shorthand lesson first 17.15–19.15, then our typing lesson 19.15–21.15. Afterwards, we would decide to either get the bus home, or spend our bus fare on some chips and walk the three miles home.

One day, Verity said "Colin's got a mate, he's called Carl and he looks like Donny Osmond. D'you fancy meeting him?"

"If he looks like Donny Osmond, too right I do!" I said. So next college night, the two of them were waiting outside for us. Oh my gawd, Verity wasn't kidding. He was the spitting image of Donny Osmond. Verity and Colin walked ahead after introductions and Carl and I chatted nervously. He was shy and quiet, totally different to Terry which was a very nice contrast. We all decided to walk home as it was a lovely evening. About half way home Carl took hold of my hand and we walked in comfortable companionship the rest of the way. My second boyfriend had arrived.

Going to the disco with Carl was a lot nicer than with Terry. Carl never got into fights and was very well behaved. But after a while we seemed to get bored with each other and he gradually stopped meeting me from college. I didn't shed any tears that time.

I decided I would like a Saturday job. Verity wanted to be a hairdresser and had a Saturday job at a hairdresser's in town, so I began asking around. I was offered a job in the Co-op Departmental Store in town. The same store Mum used to work at, but I was in the food hall. I was employed to fill the shelves. I absolutely loved the job and looked forward to every Saturday.

There were two young boys working there, both called Joe: one was nicknamed little Joe so as to distinguish them. Both boys were very nice, but I fancied one in particular. One of the older ladies that I worked with came over to me one day as I was stacking the shelves.

"Joe wants to go out with you," she said quietly in my ear.

"Which one?" I enquired.

"Both of them!" she laughed.

Well now I felt bad about having to choose, but I couldn't go out with both of them, so I guess a decision had to be made. It wasn't too difficult as they were both extremely nice. I definitely fancied one in particular more than the other though.

"Little Joe," I said.

"Ok I'll tell them," she said, hurrying away.

I continued doing my job while waiting for her to return. With her as a go-between, a date was arranged for that night after work to go to Top Rank in town. Joe was very shy, as I was, but we had a great evening.

"He's very quiet," I told Mum and Dad later.

Joe had seen me home and come in for a cup of tea with us before setting off for his home.

"Well, what d'you want?" said dad "Shouting from the rooftops?" he quipped.

Good old Dad, he could always make me laugh, and make everything right. Joe and I went out together for quite a long while, but again it became boring so we drifted apart.

CHAPTER 9

I was sitting my CSEs at school, and one day Mum came up with an idea.

"You know, with your shorthand and typing skills, you could join a temping agency and earn yourself a bit more money in the school holidays."

I looked at her thoughtfully.

"Yes, that's a good idea," I agreed.

So putting the plan into action I went along to a temping agency in town. I told the lady in the agency all that I had achieved at night school and the CSEs I was in the middle of sitting, and although she didn't give much away I came away feeling quite hopeful. About six weeks later I received a phone call. Could I work for two weeks in the school holidays in a typing pool at the airport where Mum worked? Perfect. It was only a stone's throw away from my house. I went along on the day feeling extremely nervous. After all I was still only fifteen. The head of the typing pool was quite strict, but at the same time she was extremely nice and I liked her straight away. There was one shorthand typist there and I chatted to her while she gave me a few tips. There were audio typists and copy typists too. I settled down to the work, and found the whole experience fantastic. I went there as a copy typist but our head of department let me have a go at audio typing. It wasn't as easy as it sounds, as you have to think about punctuation while listening to the dictation and typing it at the same time. It wasn't like typing on a computer: on a typewriter, you made a mistake and you started again.

Now I, after all was my dad's daughter, and taking after him I loved to joke around and make people laugh. I discovered that I had a talent for impersonating Frank Spencer, a character from 'Some Mothers Do 'Ave 'Em', and I exercised this talent quite frequently. Mum and Dad found it hilarious and unashamedly encouraged me. In the office I started coming out with quips and mannerisms from this great man, and very soon had the whole typing pool in an uproar.

"Settle down everyone, there's work to be done," our head of department would say, trying to hide a smile behind her hand.

Suffice it to say, every time that typing pool needed a temp, I was sent for.

One day the agency phoned me up. I was sixteen by now.

"Look, Glynis. The airport manager's secretary has gone off on sick leave. He needs a temp for two weeks. I've absolutely no one that is available to do it. All my temps are booked at present. Now I know this is a bit advanced for you, but do you think you could handle it just for two weeks?"

"ME?" I croaked. "Are you kidding? I can't be the airport manager's secretary!"

"Yes you can." She said calmly. I went silent for a minute.

"Well, ok. I'll try," I said apprehensively

"Good girl," she replied. "I've told the airport manager that you are only sixteen and he thinks you will cope. He's ever so nice, you don't have to worry."

"Right!" I said. "When do I have to go there?"

"Monday morning. You have to go to the other side of the airport, to where the hangars are. There's a couple of hut type buildings. You report there."

Oh my gawd. What have I taken on, I thought. Mum and Dad were impressed.

"An airport manager's secretary at your age!" Mum said enthusiastically.

"It's only for two weeks," I said, but I was scared to death.

Mum had to phone the headmaster at school to ask his permission, as it was term time.

"As long as it doesn't interfere with any of her exams," he said. "After all, it is furthering her career isn't it."

I set off for the far end of the airport on the Monday morning. Situated there were two very long huts – that was the only way you could describe them really. One of the pilots was walking towards one of the huts. He was quite young, in his late twenties, I would say.

"Can I help you?" he asked when he got to where I was standing.

"I'm a temp. I'm looking for the airport manager," I replied.

"Follow me, I'll show you where to go."

He led me to the second hut. Inside, there was a long corridor. Two offices led off it first, then it went into a large area which was the airport passenger lounge. He popped his head round the first door.

"This is the airport manager's office, but he's not there at the moment. You take a seat in there," he said pointing to the other office. "He won't be long."

A few moments later in walked the airport manager. What a nice man he was. He couldn't have made me feel more welcome and the patience of the man was incredible considering his extremely stressful job. I had a wonderful two weeks. This was the first time I had to use my shorthand actually in a job situation and a couple of times I couldn't quite decipher an odd word that I'd taken down.

"Don't worry dear. We'll work it out together," he would say patiently.

The pilot I had spoken to on my first day was very good to me. He showed me around some of the aircrafts. These planes weren't for commercial use, they were privately owned by the rich. I met a few of them while they were waiting in the passenger lounge. Part of my job was to keep the lounge neat and tidy, a job I quite enjoyed; it was a break from typing and of course trying to decipher my shorthand. One day, my favourite pilot popped into the office.

"D'you fancy a run out to Elstree Airport with me in your lunch break? I'll even buy you lunch."

An offer I couldn't possibly refuse. The ride to Elstree in his open top sports car was, shall we say, quite an experience. To say he drove fast would be an understatement. My hair was standing up in all directions upon our arrival. I looked like I'd been dragged through a hedge backwards and very strongly resembled a smcarecrow. Not a good image for an airport manager's secretary I have to say. That was some wind when you're belting down the road in an open top sports car I can tell you. I was a little shaky as we arrived outside Elstree Airport Hangars. It wasn't the easiest car to get out of either.

"Come on, we'll head for the canteen and I'll buy you lunch as promised," he said. Funnily enough, my appetite had completely gone, but I followed him anyway. Regardless of the wind almost blowing my hair away, I'd had a lovely time with a very charming pilot. Having said that, I certainly didn't want to repeat the experience.

The two weeks came to an end and I returned to school. I received a glowing report from the airport manager and so from then on, until I started full-time employment, every time the airport manager's secretary was absent, I was asked for.

CHAPTER 10

The time came for me to finally leave school, although the last two years of school had been quite acceptable. As well as Verity, I had made a couple of other very nice friends: Marian, a Spanish girl with whom I shared needlework classes, and Sophia, my commerce classmate. Marian came for a trip out to Blackpool to see the illuminations with us one day and we had made Mum and Dad laugh when our very long, shared scarf, a large gust of wind and a revolving door made for hilarious viewing. Marian sadly moved back to Spain after leaving school. We wrote to each other for a while but eventually lost touch. I am still in touch with Sophia and Verity to this day. I couldn't believe my final day had come at last, and it was with no hesitation that I held my head up high and walked out through the school gates for the very last time. I didn't look back.

Every year, the airport took on six girls to train them to be secretaries and I was lucky enough to be offered one of those places. One day a week we were sent to college to study shorthand, typing, English and office practice. George Stephenson's College in Water Lane was a lovely college, very modern, and I very much enjoyed Mondays spent there. We had a rest room where we all went at lunch times to chat and listen to records. A song that was frequently played was 'Everything I Own' by Ken Booth. This song will always remind me of my wonderful college days. Of course I no longer had my Saturday job at the Co-op or my temping job, so I was able to concentrate on my first full-time job.

A few of the secretaries at the airport got together once a week to go to a keep fit class. One of them asked me to go along with them one evening.

"Oh, but I'm not much of a keep fit fanatic," I replied.

"You don't have to be. We just go to have a laugh and get a bit of exercise. We go to the pub afterwards," said one of the girls in the typing pool.

"Well I'm not much of a drinker either."

"That's ok, you can have orange juice," she said

"Erm."

"Oh go on, we all want you to come 'cos you make us laugh!" she persisted.

"All right then, I will," I said.

I figured it couldn't be that bad if they ALL went. We got to the class and started warming up with exercises. I could feel all the secretaries watching me, waiting for me to start my Frank Spencer nonsense. I didn't like to disappoint them.

"Hmm, I can't do this, I'm getting all harassed," I drawled in my Frank Spencer voice, while acting out all his mannerisms.

Of course everyone burst out laughing, which was like fuel to a fire to me, and I continued my entertaining. I just couldn't help myself; hearing the laughter, well it gave me such a buzz. After the class we would get changed and go to the pub where I would get up and entertain everyone again. This became a weekly ritual, going to a different pub every time. One night after the class, a young girl came up to me. She held out a small book and pen towards me.

"Please can I have your autograph?" she asked.

"You want my autograph?" I was puzzled.

"Yes, my mum said you're gonna be famous one day."

NO WAY. I was flabbergasted. I could honestly say my flabber had never been so gasted. But I have to say, I got a real kick out of it, and I signed her book for her.

As a trainee secretary, part of the training was to move around all the different offices within the airport learning all the different departments. So my keep fit mates never knew exactly where I would be each week. So, as my mum still worked at the airport, they would all phone her up to see if I was going to keep fit. If Mum told them I wasn't going for some reason, then they wouldn't go either. It was crazy but they felt it wasn't as much fun without my daft escapades.

It was my eighteenth birthday. Mum and Dad asked me if I would like a party or whether I would prefer a bigger present instead. I chose the bigger present, a music centre. It was lovely, and with all the birthday money I received from various relations, I bought a cabinet to put it on. However, a celebration was in order, and a large number of my mates came out with me to Baileys nightclub. There were always famous entertainers on there. Verity and I went there a lot, and this night Gene Pitney was the star. He was brilliant of course and we were having a wonderful evening when I heard the compère say "I believe we have a Frank Spencer impersonator in the audience tonight. Would you come up on the stage, Glynis?"

I froze. They have got to be kidding. I knew this was the work of my mates. They all pushed me towards the stage, and somehow I managed to climb up the steps onto the stage where the compare took my hand.

"Hello, Glynis. Now we've been told you do a pretty good impression of Frank Spencer, so it's over to you."

He handed me the microphone, and I couldn't do anything else but perform. It was all a bit of a blur after that, and with the lights on me I couldn't see much of the huge amount of people there, but I heard the intoxicating sound of laughter and then the compère was back at my side. The lights went up a bit and I caught sight of the audience, I began to panic slightly at the amount of people that were actually looking at me, but the compère took control.

"That's brilliant darling," he said as he steadied me. One of the dancing girls came out carrying an ice bucket with a bottle of Champagne in it. She handed it to the compère, and he handed it to me. I squinted as the flash of a camera went off and I took the ice bucket from him.

"Happy birthday, Glynis," he said and he kissed me on my cheek.

"Thank you," was all I could manage to say, and I made my way back to my friends.

The rest of the evening went very well and I eventually went home on cloud nine. Mum and Dad were of course waiting up for me, and they both looked up searching my face for clues of having had a good evening.

"It was fantastic," I said dreamily, waving my empty bottle of Champagne in the air. I told them all about the evening, showing them the photographs taken of me on the stage.

"And then Gene Pitney signed my birthday key for me," I said excitedly. "He was brilliant."

Life went on pretty smoothly until one day Dad announced that Odhams, the printing firm he worked for, was closing and they were asking for voluntary redundancies. Now Dad had reached the top of his career in the printing trade and apart from getting to Fleet Street, he couldn't get any further. So maybe it was time he had a career change.

"How do you fancy moving to Barrow-in-Furness?" he suddenly came out with one day. Dad had always been impulsive, so I was quite used to these sudden announcements, but not a lot of thought was needed here.

"Oooh yes!" Mum and I shouted out together.

"Now, you have to think about this, love," he said to me. "You have a good job at the airport and you've got to consider that. If you want to stay in Watford we can arrange somewhere for you to live quite easily.

"Are you mad? I want to go to Barrow-in Furness-with you," I replied with no hesitation.

We had all fallen in love with that lovely little town a long time ago. Dad drove Mum and me up to Barrow-in-Furness to look for a property. He had to work, so he returned to Watford and left us to narrow down a couple of properties for him to view. We stayed with one of our distant relatives Ellen and Clive and their three children Jay, Isaac and Amy. Auntie Ellen, as I called her, drove us around to view various houses. We had a great time narrowing it down to two houses for Dad to look at: one in Cheltenham Street and one in Smeaton Street. When Dad returned a week later, a choice was made. I had really set my heart on Cheltenham Street, but Mum and Dad decided to buy the house in Smeaton Street. The value of the house was much less than half of the value of our house in Watford, so Mum and Dad had enough money to be able to keep us all comfortably until we were all able to get jobs.

CHAPTER 11

It was January 1976. The large removal van pulled up outside our house in Ridgehust Avenue. It had Barrow-in-Furness in large letters along the side. Two men jumped down from the cab, and we went outside to greet them.

"Hello," said Mum.

"A removal to go to Barrow-in-Furness?" one of them said looking at the sheet of paper he was holding.

"Yes, that's right," Mum replied.

"Great, I hope you know where the kettle is. Two sugars in mine, thanks," he said cheekily, with a big smile on his face.

His mate was shaking his head apologetically. Mum and Dad had got estimates from various removal firms and it was far cheaper to get a firm from the north of England than it was to use a Watford firm. So, here they were.

They got straight down to loading the van, while Mum as instructed, went to put the kettle on. A few minutes later she appeared holding a tray with mugs of steaming tea and a variety of biscuits in a tin.

"Come on," she said. "Have a break for a minute."

"Don't need telling twice," said cheeky chappie. You could tell by his physique that he hadn't gone short of tea and biscuits during his career. Taking their mugs of tea and helping themselves to the biscuits they sat down for a rest.

"Are you looking forward to moving up north?" Cheeky chappie asked me.

"Yes, I am," I replied.

We all chatted for a while as he told me about life in Barrow-in-Furness and all that went on there. He told me there were fantastic night clubs, and that all the stars performed in them. I later discovered that the man had been highly prone to exaggeration, but he was nice enough, so I suppose he could be forgiven.

A few hours later, the large van was fully loaded and the men slammed the back doors shut.

"Right, well we'll see you up north then."

"Yes," said Dad. "See you there."

Once we had checked over the house to make sure we hadn't left anything behind, Dad locked up for the last time in Watford. We all got into the car, cat and dog included, and I looked out of the car window, taking one, kind of sad, last look at the house, reflecting on the events of the past eight years.

When I left my job at the airport my wonderful workmates had made a collection and bought me a present: a lovely big red jewellery box. Also, one of the draughtsmen had drawn a large picture of me inside a leaving card, and they presented it all to me. The picture drawn was a cartoon of me, surrounded by various significant things in my life. Quite brilliant, and everyone had signed it. I have kept it ever since.

We travelled all through the night and arrived in Barrow-in-Furness early the next morning. It wasn't long before our cheery removal men arrived.

"Good morning!" they called out as they walked through the open door of our new home.

"It's ok, I know exactly where the tea making box is. I'll get that off the van first," said cheeky chappie.

After a welcome cup of tea, and biscuits, the men skilfully

went to work filling our home with all our possessions. We had now arrived in the north of England.

Our lifestyle changed dramatically. We had no jobs for a start. Mum and Dad, after selling the house in Watford and purchasing this house, had enough money to keep us until we gained employment, but there were one or two things we had to purchase like bedroom furniture, as all of our wardrobes in Watford had been fitted. We went along to a little furniture shop in town to pick out some new wardrobes.

"What d'you think of that?" said Dad pointing to a large white wardrobe fitment with louvre doors either side of a dressing table.

"Ooh it's lovely," I cooed.

"Would you like it for your room?" he asked.

"Cor blimey, I'd love it," I quickly replied. So Mum and Dad chose all the other furniture that they needed, and also some that they didn't actually need, like a new three piece suite in light brown fake leather which was extremely comfortable, and a lovely round, teak dining table with four chairs, which they bought just for the hell of it, and then we went home.

Once the house was sorted, we went along to the Labour Exchange to look for work. I quite fancied a change of career, maybe working in a hotel. Well let's face it, working at an airport was definitely going to be out of the question. So the three of us started applying for jobs. I managed to get a job first, in a hotel, which I was very excited about. It wasn't in Barrow though, it was in Grasmere, not too far away but it meant living in. Apart from staying with my nana and grandad for a week or two every summer, and that holiday to Swanage with the school, I had never been away from Mum and Dad. So I was a little apprehensive, but at the same time very keen to start.

Mum and Dad drove me up to Grasmere on my starting day, and I was shown to a building within the grounds of the hotel. It was a converted stable, and although the view from the window was lovely, with sheep directly outside, the actual accommodation left a lot to be desired. However I figured that as I would be working in the hotel most of the time and going home on my days off, it probably wouldn't matter that much. Mum and Dad looked around the minimal furnishings. I could tell they were not impressed.

"Hmm, well we can bring some bits and pieces to make it a bit more homely, I suppose," said Mum.

"Yes, it'll be fine," I agreed.

"It's awful," stated Dad bluntly.

He never did mince his words. I decided to make the best of it and I unpacked my case. I was to start my training the next day, along with the rest of the staff being taken on. At first I liked it very much. The two weeks' training was great, they taught us how to carry four plates at a time for waitressing, how to change a plug and all sorts of other things relating to the hotel. We were treated to a film showing us how the hotel was built and started, with the Jim Reeves song 'Welcome To My World' playing all the way through it. It was very interesting. Out of all of us, there were only two of us that had any office experience, so we were allocated the reception between us, but we worked in the dining area and the housekeeping side too. In the evening we had to wear long dresses, which quite frankly were a pain in the neck. I was always tripping over the hem

One evening we had an important person dining in, and I was chosen to serve him. To say I was nervous about this prospect was an understatement, and inevitably I managed to make a pig's ear of it. While serving up the gentleman's main course, placing various vegetables upon his plate, I accidently dropped some carrots right into his lap. OH NO! I just froze. I clearly couldn't pick them up, but what on earth should I do? They didn't teach us that one during training.

"I'm so sorry," I said meekly.

Well, what else could I say? But the gentleman was wonderful. He couldn't have been nicer about it.

"It's all right dear," he said, lightly patting my hand. "You walk away and I'll pick them up when you've gone."

Well, what can I say but the man was a true gent. Needless to say, I was on washing-up duties for quite a while after that.

The dampness of my living quarters began to take its toll on me. I wasn't eating much either as we didn't get our evening meal until after all the diners had gone, which was around 23.30, but this was a little late for me. I was so tired that I would go straight to bed. I was slim when I started the job as all my puppy fat had dropped off of me long ago, but now I was, shall we say well and truly on the skinny side. We worked split shifts, starting at 7.30, having about three hours off in the afternoon, then back to work at 17.00. I lost a lot of weight, going down to six stone, and I became quite ill.

Dad always came to fetch me home for my one and a half days off each week, and Mum would get as much food down me as she possibly could before Dad had to take me back to the hotel. I became quite weak, and one day I went down to the phone box to phone Mum and Dad, as I did every day. Mum and Dad worried and liked to know I was ok. Mum answered the phone and she seemed quite anxious.

"Go back to the hotel, love. Your dad's on his way to see you. We want you to come home."

I suddenly perked up and after putting the phone down I raced round to the hotel, to find Dad parking the car.

"Watchya Dad!" I said happily.

"Come on, love. Get your things. You're coming home."

The relief I felt was tremendous. Although I wanted to work, I just felt so ill all the time. When I had packed my case, and gathered all my things together I went outside to find Dad. I could see him talking to the owner of the hotel over on the newly cut lawn. When I say 'talking' what I actually mean is the owner was talking but Dad was shouting at him.

"But she has to work her notice, she can't just walk out," the owner was saying to Dad.

"She ain't working no notice 'cos she's too ill. If you treated your employees better, this wouldn't be 'appening," said Dad, shaking his fist in the air at him. "I'm taking 'er home and you can stuff your job where the sun don't shine," he added.

I was impressed. That's my Dad!

CHAPTER 12

It was the summer of 1976. We hadn't had a summer as hot as this one for a very long time, and there I was out of work. It doesn't get any more perfect than that. I got stronger and stronger relaxing and strolling around the magnificent park with my trusty friend, Shep. Dad decided to trade our car in for a caravanette and we would go to the coast road or up to the lakes for picnics.

After a while, Dad was offered a job as a security guard in a local supermarket and as I had learnt to drive back in Watford, I decided that I would like a little car of my own.

Dad arrived home from work one hot Saturday afternoon in July having been on the early shift.

"There's a bloke at work who's selling his car. It might be worth looking at," he said.

"Ooh yeah. When can we go and see it?" I asked excitedly.

"No time like the present," he laughed. Mum came out of the kitchen wiping her hands on her apron.

"I'm just getting the dinner ready, so don't be long," she said.

"No we won't be long," said dad.

When we got there, the bloke in question, the tyre bay manager, was there alone.

"Where's that car you're selling?" Dad said to him.

"My apprentice has just taken it out for a test drive, he'll be back in a minute," he replied.

I couldn't wait to see the car, so I sat on the wall outside to watch out for it coming back while dad stood chatting to him. Next thing, there was a screeching of tyres and a white Cortina came hurtling into the tyre bay. A young bloke with long shoulder length blond hair got out and, hitching up his oil stained trousers, he sauntered over to where his boss and my Dad were standing. I sat and watched them talking for a minute, and I saw Dad point over to me, so I jumped down from the wall and made my way over to the car. Casually looking it over, I remember thinking, the car is lovely but I'm glad he doesn't come with it, referring to the long-haired apprentice. I thought he was a bit scruffy looking. I looked at Dad, as he was inspecting the engine. After a close look all over he looked at me shaking his head.

"I'm not sure it's right for you love," he said sadly.

I was so disappointed. Long-haired apprentice looked at me, then turned to Dad.

"I'll look out for a car suitable for your daughter," he said.

"Yeah, ok. Thanks," said Dad. Then he started talking to the boss again. I went and sat back on the wall to wait for dad. Long-haired apprentice came over to me.

"What sort a car you after then?" he asked.

"Dunno really, I ain't fussy. One with four wheels I s'pose," I said flippantly.

"Five!" he said.

"What?"

"Five wheels. You need one to steer it with too," he said smiling at me.

I laughed half-heartedly. I realised he was just trying to be nice, but I was still disappointed and felt a little grumpy. I suddenly remembered what Mum had said about not being long, I thought if I don't say something Dad will stand there talking all night, so I jumped down off the wall.

"Come on, Dad. Mum will be cross if we're too long."

Dad looked at his watch.

"Oh my gawd, I didn't realise the time. See yer later," he said, waving goodbye.

Around 19.00 that same evening, I was running a bath when the doorbell rang. Dad went to the front door. I could hear talking and whoever it was had come into the house. My curiosity got the better of me so I turned the taps off and went downstairs. It was long-haired apprentice with his mate. They were both all dressed up for a night out and were looking very smart, totally different to when I had seen him this afternoon. I was puzzled. What on earth were they doing here at this time on a Saturday night?

"Darren's come round about work," Dad explained. So Darren, it seemed was long-haired apprentice.

"Oh!" I replied.

Darren smiled at me. I smiled back and I turned to go back upstairs. I heard Dad tell them to sit down, and then he asked them if they wanted a cup of tea or coffee.

"Coffee please," said Darren.

His mate said he would have the same. I decided to give up on the bath for now, so I pulled the plug out and went downstairs. We all had a good laugh that evening, I ended up getting my Frank Spencer outfit on and entertaining our guests. There were literally tears of laughter running down Darren's face as he and his mate roared with laughter. At the end of the night, many hours later, Darren asked Dad if he and Mum fancied going out for a drink the following night. Dad looked at Mum.

"That would be nice," she said.

"You come too," Darren said to me. "We'll have a game of pool."

"Haven't got a clue how to play pool," I replied.

"I'll teach you," he said smiling. "See you tomorrow."

"Ok," I shrugged.

After they had gone, I turned to Dad.

"So what did they actually come for, Dad?"

"Dunno really, something about a key I think. Although I suspect he really came to see you."

"Me, why?"

"'Cos he fancies you, I s'pose."

"No, I don't think so," I said shaking my head.

"Well, I'm pretty sure he doesn't fancy me," Dad said.

The following evening Darren turned up at our house promptly at 19.00.

"Where's your mate?" asked Mum

"Oh, he's not coming," Darren said looking at me. I caught Dad giving Mum a knowing look.

Darren directed Dad to a lovely little pub just outside Barrow, in a place called Newton. Settling down with our drinks, Darren turned to me.

"D'you fancy a game of pool then? I'll show you how to play."

I looked over to where the big pool table stood in the corner.

"I'll never get up on that table," I said. Darren laughed.

"You don't get up there," he said.

"Well, ok then. I'll have a go," I said hesitantly.

Once Darren had set up the table, he gestured for me to go first. I leaned over the table aiming the peculiar looking stick at the ball, but I missed it by a mile. Darren smiled as I stood there scowling at it.

"I'll show you," he said patiently and leaned over with me, guiding my hands, showing me how to hold the silly looking stick. It was all too complicated for me and I quickly got bored with it.

"D'you wanna sit down now?" said Darren, after he had won the game.

"Yeah, ok," I replied not being able to hide the sound of relief in my voice.

Darren laughed. We put the sticks down and went over to Mum and Dad.

"How about darts?" asked Darren.

"I've never played that either," I replied

"Come on, it's easy," he said. I must admit I liked that game a little better and at one point I actually hit the dart board. But everyone in the pub started to look a little uneasy so I thought I had better sit down for safety's sake. The rest of the evening went well and again we had a good laugh. Later on in the evening Darren took me to one side.

"Will you go out with me tomorrow night?" he asked.

I looked across to where Mum and Dad were sitting.

"No, I don't mean with your Mum and Dad. Just you and me."

"I dunno," I said, hesitating.

"Oh go on, I'll take you to my local," he persisted.

I figured I may as well. I had nothing better to do.

"Ok then."

I decided he was, after all good company.

The following evening we went to Darren's local pub. It was actually a hotel, but we went to the bar end at the side of the building. The bar was full of very nice people and we had a very enjoyable evening. The actual place was quite rough and ready, a far cry from the places I was used to in Watford, but the people were extremely nice and they made me feel very welcome. As Darren walked me home that night, he took my hand and asked if he could see me again.

"Yeah, ok. But not tomorrow," I said elusively.

Darren looked disappointed, so I quickly said, "Maybe at the weekend."

He seemed cheered by that and smiled.

I started going out with him more and more. I really enjoyed his company and pretty soon found myself falling in love with him. However, I was still looking for a car to buy, and one day Dad said he had seen a little Ford Anglia for sale.

"It's quite old," he said. "But we can go and have a look."

Darren came along with us as he knew a little bit about cars. The three of us paraded around the car inspecting it closely.

"Yes, it seems sound enough," said Darren.

I began to get excited.

"Can I buy it then?" I asked Dad.

"Well, it's up to you. If Darren thinks it's ok, I don't see why not."

At last I was going to own my own car. Admittedly there was more rust on it than paint, but it was all mine and I was proud of it. What paintwork was left was white with a red stripe along the side.

One Saturday Darren asked me if I would like to go and meet his parents.

"Ok," I shrugged.

So the next day he took me to a large house where his parents lived. Part of the house was his Dad's barber shop. His dad was one of the best barbers in Barrow, and a nicer couple you couldn't possibly meet. I loved them straight away. Mary and Derek were wonderful and they made me feel very welcome. Darren had an older sister, Jessica, who was married to Tony. They had two children, Gary and Kerry, and Jessica was expecting twins. The whole family was quite perfect, and I felt very comfortable in their company. It was a funny coincidence that my very first friend back in Rugby was called Darren and his mum was Mary also.

My search for a job was still ongoing and as I attended yet another interview, this time for a sewing machinist job, the very nice manager Mr Leicester interviewing me was sitting looking at all my certificates for shorthand and typing... etc.

"Well, I really don't think you are sewing machinist material," he said.

I wanted to laugh at the pun, but as he wasn't smiling, I thought I had better not.

"No, looking at these, I think you're more suited to office work," he continued. "We have someone leaving in a couple of weeks, would you be interested in working in our office instead?"

"Yes please," I replied.

"Ok, well I'll be in touch in a couple of weeks' time and we'll fix a starting date."

And with that, he stood up and held his hand out to me. I also got up and we shook hands. I was over the moon. It looked like I was going to be employed again shortly. I took great joy in telling Mum and Dad when I got home, and later I related the events to Darren.

Sticking to his word, Mr Leicester sent me a letter offering me a job as a clerical assistant and gave me a date to start. The job was quite varied: as well as typing, I worked out the machinists' daily bonuses which I found quite interesting. There were two separate factories. I started working at one of them and then was asked to move to the other factory's office.

It was October, and Darren and I had been going out together for three months. As we were walking to our local pub Darren suddenly stopped, faced me and took hold of my hands.

"You know I'm in love with you, don't you?" he asked me.

"Yes, I s'pose," I shrugged.

He searched my face for a clue as to what I was thinking. To be honest, I couldn't be doing with all this slushy stuff. I just wanted to go to the pub. Since Darren had introduced me to lager I had become quite partial to the drink, and right now my mouth felt extremely dry.

"Shall we go to the pub now," I urged him, taking a step forward.

"Wait!" he put his hand on my arm and steered me round to face him again. He was looking quite nervous.

"Will you marry me?" he blurted out.

Oh my gawd, I couldn't breathe. I felt in a bit of a panic. What did he have to go and say THAT for? I was perfectly happy the way we were.

"Well?" he prompted me. I didn't know what to say.

"I'll think about it," was all I could manage.

I knew that wasn't the answer he was hoping for, but it was so unexpected and I wasn't prepared. I needed time to think. The poor man looked puzzled by my answer, but he quickly recovered.

"Ok, I'll ask you again later," he said calmly, and we carried on walking to the pub.

We had a couple of drinks of lager and I began to feel a little calmer as I tried to sort out my feelings. I asked myself, what would life be like without Darren? And I had to admit, the prospect was not appealing.

It was around 22.00, the pub was full and Darren got up, turned around and got down on one knee. I felt more prepared that time and when he popped the question for the second time, I simply said, "Yes."

Everyone in the pub cheered and Darren drew me to my feet and hugged me.

"Thank God. You certainly didn't make that easy." He laughed, and I laughed too.

After Darren had walked me home that night we stood on the doorstep.

"I'll come round to your house tomorrow and ask your Dad's permission to marry you."

I thought that was a nice touch.

"He'll appreciate that," I smiled.

When I got in, Mum and Dad were watching TV. I told them about the proposal. Mum was pleased but Dad just muttered something under his breath. He didn't seem impressed.

The following evening Darren came round to ask Dad's permission, but Dad was clearly not going to co-operate.

"Gerry, I'd like to ask..."

"I know exactly who the murderer is here," interrupted Dad pointing to the TV.

"Gerry, listen. Darren's trying to ask you something," said Mum.

It was quite painful as Dad continued to evade the question. Eventually the question was asked and Dad reluctantly grunted a 'yeah'.

"We'll go to the jewellers next Saturday and you can choose an engagement ring," Darren said later, as we were saying goodnight on the doorstep.

In the jewellers, the assistant measured my finger with a ring sizer.

"Good gracious, your fingers are very small, aren't they? I don't think we have any rings in a size G," he said. "But don't worry, whichever one you choose we can send it away to make it your size."

"It's ok, we're not getting engaged till your birthday. There's plenty of time," said Darren.

I nodded and began looking through the many exquisite rings on display. I chose a solitaire diamond. It was quite pricey, but Darren assured me money was no object when it came to choosing the right ring.

"It'll be about two weeks getting altered," said the jeweller as he was writing all the details on the order form. When we went to collect it two weeks later, I tried it on in the shop.

"Ooh it's lovely," I crooned. I didn't want to take it off.

"Well, I know we were gonna get engaged on your birthday, but as it's not far off you may as well leave it on," said Darren.

I had bought him an identity bracelet with his name engraved on it to mark the occasion, and he too was trying it on as it had also returned complete with engraving. So that was it, we were engaged.

Shortly after that, Mum got a job in the shipyard. So now we were all employed. Darren's boss had left, and Darren had been made up to manager of the tyre bay. However it was still not a well-paid job and as we were saving up for a deposit to buy a house, Mum suggested Darren also applied to work in the shipyard.

"It's much better pay, so you'll be able to save more," she said logically. So Darren put an application into the shipyard personnel department and very soon was offered a job as a crane driver.

Christmas was just around the corner and Dad had just bought a Scalextric. He and Darren set it all up in the lounge, filling the whole room with nowhere left to walk. Mum and I had to climb over the furniture to get to the kitchen. Not ideal but necessary, apparently. We were informed that if we thought they were going to put their new toy away, just so as we could walk on the floor, well, we were very sadly mistaken, but we all had a good laugh and a great Christmas was had by all.

On leaving Watford, I'd waved a tearful goodbye to my old faithful friend Miss Green. I had promised her that I would write to her often, and I had kept my promise. There was a definite hole in my Sundays where I used to visit her, but I had kept her informed of my every move as I went along. She was pleased when I told her about Darren. She always replied to my letters. Miss Green was approaching eighty years old and was quite set in her ways when it came to fandangled gadgets (as she put it) like telephones, so I could only keep in touch by letter.

Imagine my distress, when after Christmas, the card and letter I had sent to her before Christmas, was returned to me, along with a note from her neighbour informing me of the very sad news that Miss Green had passed away. I shed more than a few tears for that wonderful old lady and wished I could have been with her at the sad ending of her life.

About a year later we had enough money saved up to put down a deposit on a house, and we set out to find our ideal home. We looked at quite a few two bedroomed houses and finally settled on one in Kitchener street over on Walney Island. We got a mortgage with no problems and even had enough to get central heating installed. Then we set to work decorating it. Our wedding was planned for 13th May 1978, so our lives were full of wedding plans and making our little house into a home.

Unfortunately, three weeks before our wedding, tragedy struck. My grandad Saunders collapsed and was taken to hospital. We all travelled down to Gillingham to see him but when we got there, he was unconscious and the doctor sadly informed us that he would not recover. We were devastated. My beloved grandad was not going to see me get married after all. This brought a sadness to the day, but I hoped he was looking down as we sang his favourite hymn, 'All Things Bright and Beautiful'.

My good friend Verity had travelled up with her husband. She was expecting their first child so I really appreciated the effort that she made to be there, as I did all my family and friends who had also travelled up for our special day.

I had two bridesmaids, Amy and Noreen. Amy was of course Auntie Ellen and Uncle Clive's daughter and Noreen was the daughter of Mum and Dad's friends, Natalie and Arnold from Letchworth. They had two other children, Dennis and Marlene. They were actually a Scottish family but like us, had moved to Letchworth for the work. Amy and Noreen were dressed in long flowing pink dresses and looked absolutely enchanting. I, of course, wore the full bridal dress and veil, and Darren wore a blue suit. Tony, Darren's brother-in-law, was his best man.

The whole day went wonderfully, as I became Mrs Ellison. Darren and I travelled in a black Limousine from St George's Church down to The Old Mill at Bardsea for the reception. Later on it was back to Walney Island to a room above a pub for our evening do. I changed out of my wedding dress into a cream coloured jumpsuit and we danced to 'A little bit more' by Dr Hook.

Later, near the end of the evening, I looked across the room and saw Dad sitting on his own in the corner, looking a little sad. Mum was chatting to some friends. I made my way over to where Dad was, and sat down beside him.

"You ok, Dad?" I asked.

"Yeah ok, love," he said forcing a smile. But I knew he wasn't.

"It was a great day, wasn't it?" I said.

"Yes, it was, love. It went very well."

"Ya know, I won't be far away, Dad."

"Yeah I know love. It won't be the same without you though," he said sadly.

I felt a little choked, so I just patted his hand. At the end of the evening Dad insisted on driving Darren and me to our new home. As we stood outside our little house waving goodnight to Mum and Dad, a sudden sadness enveloped me as the thought struck me that this moment was the end of an era.

CHAPTER 13

About a month after our wedding, Darren and I were out for a Sunday drive. We often went up to the lakes, liking the tranquil atmosphere there. As we were driving home through Pennington, we noticed a lot of dogs being paraded around the field in front of Pennington Hall.

"Shall we stop and see what's going on?" I said.

"Yeah, ok," said Darren.

We got out of the car and made our way through the crowd of people inside the hall. Suddenly I stopped still and pointed across the hall.

"Oh my gawd, look at the size of that dog," I said astounded by the huge beast.

It was a Great Dane. We went over to get a closer look at this magnificent animal.

"Oh Darren, we've got to have one of these dogs," I stated, stroking the beautiful dog.

"He's lovely, isn't he?" said Darren.

I eventually tore myself away from the gorgeous dog but one thing was apparent, I was definitely going to own a Great Dane, and soon.

Two months later we were travelling home from Yorkshire with our Great Dane puppy. Darren thought of his name. Ben.

"Let's go and show both our parents," I said.

We hadn't told them we were getting him yet. We thought we would surprise them.

"What breed do you think he is?" I asked my mum and dad.

"He looks like a Great Dane or something like that," said Dad, examining him closely.

"Yes that's right," I said. "Isn't he gorgeous?"

"D'you realise how big this dog's gonna grow?" said Dad looking slightly worried.

"Yes, he's gonna be huge," I said with a big smile.

"Well, the pair of you are barmy," said Mum. "Why can't you get a sensible sized dog?"

"He is a sensible sized dog. No one's gonna trip over HIM when he gets to be fully grown are they?" I rationalised.

"No, I'll give you that," said Dad. "No one else is gonna get in the room with him, let alone trip over him when he gets bigger."

But nothing could dampen my spirits. I was thrilled with him and so was Darren. On introducing him to Darren's parents we received a similar negative response but we didn't care, he was the cutest thing we had ever seen.

One Sunday, we were round at Mum and Dad's for a visit, when Dad suddenly came out with some devastating news.

"I've got a new job as a railway guard. But it's back down south so we're moving back to Gillingham."

"Yes we thought we could keep an eye on the two nanas and grandad. After all they're not getting any younger," said Mum.

I was speechless for a minute. Mum and Dad had never been far away from me before, but they were clearly excited about the move and I didn't want to spoil it for them, so I said with a smile, "That's great, it'll be wonderful working on the trains, Dad."

Dad had got a job in the shipyard not so long ago, but he couldn't take to it.

"Yes, I'm looking forward to it. Well, I never did like it in the shipyard. It's just not me working there. This is a good opportunity."

"When are you going?" I asked.

"Well, I'm going next week to start the job. I've put my notice in at the shipyard. Mum's staying here till the house is sold, and I'm staying with your nana Saunders till we buy one of our own.

"Oh!"

I was just trying to digest this information. Later, Darren noticed I was a bit quiet and he tried to reassure me.

"It's ok, love. You've got me, and my mum and dad are here. We'll visit your mum and dad often."

"Yes I know."

I was just being silly. This feeling of insecurity will pass.

It didn't take long for the house to sell and then Mum went too. The house next door to Nana's came up for sale in Wellington Road, and Mum and Dad decided to buy it. Mum got a job in Medway Hospital in the CSSD department and eventually they moved into the house next door.

I had reached the age of twenty-one by now, and a formal-looking envelope dropped through our letterbox addressed to Miss G Puddle. On opening it, I discovered it was from my uncle Stan's solicitors. It said they'd had a lot of trouble tracking me down, but eventually had got my address from the other brother's family, and could I get in touch to arrange payment from Uncle Stan's will. I stood staring at the letter. So here it was, the root of all that nastiness I had endured at school. I had never told Darren about any of this. He didn't have a clue that this money was coming to me. Of course with inflation it wasn't worth that much now. It had gained a little interest but even so, the amount was nowhere near what it was worth back then. Now I had to tell Darren.

"Yor kidding, right?" he laughed, when I told him about the money.

I didn't mention all the heartache that had gone with it.

"What are you gonna do with it?" he asked cheerfully.

"Dunno, haven't thought about it," I shrugged.

He looked at me as though I'd taken leave of my senses, but he didn't comment on my reaction. I replied to the letter and about three weeks later a cheque arrived for £2,400. I paid the cheque into our joint account and put it to the back of my mind.

After a few weeks had lapsed Darren approached the subject again.

"Have you decided what you wanna do with that money?

"Well, I have a little," I replied. "I was thinking maybe we could get a new sofa and a double-glazed front door, that door is awful draughty. And maybe we could get a new hall, stairs and landing carpet. That one's a bit threadbare. What d'you think?"

"Those are great ideas," said Darren.

After purchasing those things there was still some left. I told Darren I wanted to buy something to remind me of my uncle Stan, but I couldn't think what to get so I put it on hold for now.

The more Ben grew, the more destructive he became and as he was so much bigger than ordinary puppies he could have course reach so much more. He managed to destroy our new sofa. He ripped up curtains, books carpets and just about anything he could get his cheeky little puppy teeth into. Pretty soon he outgrew our little Ford Anglia and we traded it in for a green Hillman Husky. It was a very small estate car, but it gave Ben a bit more room to travel.

The destruction did not appear to be ceasing, so when Ben was eleven months old we came up with the absurd idea of getting Ben a playmate. What better way to spend the rest of Uncle Stan's money than to buy a dog, I thought, being as I enjoyed so many wonderful hours walking Laddie with Uncle Stan. I decided that this was the right decision. Yes, this was what I would buy with what was left. We saw a nineteen month old blue, female Great Dane for sale in the 'Our Dogs' magazine, so we travelled the three hour car journey with Ben in order to meet her. She was called Bonnie and she was gorgeous, to us that is. However, Ben hated her. He was ok at first, he snapped a couple of times at her on the journey home, but when it came to letting her come into our house, it was a no go situation. It was no exaggeration to say he went absolutely berserk. We had to separate them and put them in different rooms for fear of him hurting her.

"What we gonna do?" I asked Darren.

"I've no idea," he said.

It was late and we were sitting there trying to work out what to do with this feisty pair, when the telephone rang.

"Who on earth can that be at this time of night?" I said getting up to answer it.

"Hello, Mrs Ellison? This is Bonnie's previous owner. We were wondering how she's settled in."

"Not very well," I replied "Ben keeps on going for her. We've got them in different rooms at the minute."

"Well, actually we kinda regret selling her. Would it be ok if we came and collected her, and returned your cheque to you, as she's not settling?"

"Just a minute, I'll see what my husband says."

I told Darren what she had just said.

"Yes I think that will be best," he said.

She sounded relieved when I said yes they could come for her, and a while later they bounced into our house and flung their arms around her. It seemed fate had intervened and brought them back together again. They wished us luck in finding a companion for Ben.

We decided to phone the same breeder that we got Ben from. They informed us that they did have some puppies, and that they would be ready in four weeks' time. So four weeks later we travelled to Yorkshire again. There were three puppies: one male and two females.

"That one there is yours," our breeder said, pointing to the one climbing over the top of the other two.

We took her out to the car where Ben was waiting, and

introduced her to him. His reaction was good. He sniffed her all over and then settled down. She climbed all over him but he didn't seem to mind. She was only as big as Ben's head but the two of them were clearly firm friends already. We had success, and we set off to take her to her new home. I chose the name this time. I named her Zoe.

However, the destruction of our house continued, as Zoe just joined in with it. We decided to take them to dog training classes to see if we could install some good behaviour into them, and so eventually they grew out of it and settled down to be wonderful dogs. Of course the two of them soon out grew our Hillman Husky, so we traded it in for a gold Vauxhall Viva estate. But as Zoe grew to her full size, the weight of them both after a time broke the suspension, and we had to scrap the car. We then bought a purple Cortina estate. This car took their weight and it also had plenty of room for them.

We entered our Great Danes into various dog shows, gaining a few certificates for their wins. It was at this point I realised the attraction for showing smaller dogs, as when having to make the dog run for the judges, I had to run like the clappers to make my Great Danes show their running skills. One show in particular sticks in my mind: while running Ben around a field in front of the judges, Ben decided he needed a wee and promptly squatted right in the middle of his performance, he was of course oblivious to the laughter surrounding him, and casually carried on with his wee. I couldn't do anything else but wait for him to finish, because when a Great Dane wants to wee, well, there's not a lot else you CAN do. Thinking that he had blown his chances, I settled down to watch the end of the show. Imagine my surprise when the judges announced that Ben had won first prize. To this day I'm convinced that he got it on entertainment value.

The following year Darren was asked to drive a hired van for a few of his workmates doing the Keswick to Barrow walk, so I decided to attempt the forty mile walk myself. I say attempt because I only got as far as Coniston when my poor feet protested too much and I couldn't take another step. We took the two dogs with us in the van and they took it in turns to walk with me. I didn't think it fair to make them walk it all, so one rode while one walked. It was an extremely hot day and on reaching Coniston I sat down on the side of the lake and Darren took the two dogs into the lake's edge to cool them off.

"That's it," I said. "I'm done, I can't walk another step."

So I climbed into the van and rode the rest of the way with Darren and our dogs.

A couple of days later, Darren spotted an advert in the Evening Mail. It said: 'Who was the man on the Keswick to Barrow walk with the two Great Danes, spotted in Coniston Lake? Please reply.' So Darren got in touch and explained the situation to them. The next thing two reporters came round. I suddenly remembered the last experience of reporters from years ago and started to get a little jumpy.

"It's ok," they reassured me. "It's just a picture and a small article about your dogs."

"Ok," I agreed.

I figured this one was harmless, so we went into the street and they took a photograph of me walking down the road with Ben and Zoe either side of me.

So, there I was in the newspaper for a second time, this time with my Great Danes. It didn't make the front page this time and the article was entitled, 'That was no man, that was my wife.' They printed a little bit about us on the walk, and about Ben and Zoe being on it too, so I was fine with that. Quite a pleasant article.

Back in 1976 when I was applying for jobs, I had applied to Bowater Scotts, a paper factory. I had quite forgotten about the application, but now I received an invitation to attend an interview more than two years later. Very strange, I thought, but nevertheless I went to the interview and was offered a job in the Handy Andy department. It was two shifts 6.00–14.00 one week and 14.00–

22.00 the next. Each particular shift was named a different colour and I was on the red shift. I loved the job, but shortly after I started a decision was made to close the Handy Andy department. Those of us who didn't want to take redundancy were offered work in other departments. The kitchen roll department was a men-only zone, but it was decided as a trial to put just three of us women in there. Now I had to work three shifts 6.00–14.00, 14.00–22.00 and 22.00–6.00. Night shift was not good but they were a great bunch of men to work with and they made Joanie, Gloria and me very welcome. The trial was a success and we stayed.

We decided our house was now too small for our Great Danes and after looking at a few houses, we settled on a large semi-detached house in Holbeck, a fairly new estate in Barrow. So we moved to Walnut Hill, and had a lot more room for them. They even had their own bedroom, and their own single bed, which quite a few people were highly amused at. It was shortly after we moved in that Ben and Zoe proved to be quite the protectors. After finishing night shift one Tuesday morning, having been up for 24 hours I had not long been asleep when a the doorbell woke me with a start. Grabbing my dressing gown and shutting Ben and Zoe in their bedroom, I went downstairs to open the front door. Two men were standing there.

"We've come to check your double glazing," they said.

"I've just finished nights. Can it wait till another day?" I said wearily.

"Well it'll only take five minutes," said one of them.

"Well OK then," I said opening the door wider for them to come into the hallway.

They went upstairs first and I followed. However, what with getting out of bed quickly plus the lack of sleep, I promptly passed out on the landing. When I came round, imagine my surprise when upon opening my eyes, the first thing I saw was Ben's belly as he was standing over me, while growling at the two men. He had them pinned up against the wall with Zoe the other side of them preventing them from leaving.

"Er, can you call your horses off? said one of them with a panic-stricken face.

"We thought that room was the bathroom, we were trying to get you a drink of water," said the other one pointing towards my Great Danes' bedroom.

I got up onto my feet and took hold of each of their collars. I have to say, I have never seen anyone run out of a house so fast in my life, as they shouted over their shoulders, "Your double glazing's fine" and promptly disappeared out of the front door. Peace at last. Perhaps I can get some sleep now I thought.

It was carnival time and Barrow displayed the finest carnivals that I had ever seen. Some friends of ours who we had met at dog training classes asked Darren and me to dress up and go in the carnival as collectors. Darren went as a mummy and I went as a punk rocker. I had been having my hair dyed blonde recently but decided to spray a green colour onto it for the carnival. Of course I failed to read the bit on the can which does not recommend spraying it onto bleached hair, so when I went to wash it out, it would not budge. I had to go to work with green streaks in my hair. Everyone at work found this hilarious.

There was a craze of operating a CB radio going on and Darren had caught the bug. He called himself 'Skybird'. This was known as a handle. He was on this radio contraption almost non-stop. Darren started talking to a couple called Sharon and Patrick. Their handles were ' Liver Bird' and 'Cavalier'. I arrived home from a 14.00–22.00 shift one night when Darren said, "My CB friends want to meet you. D'you fancy going round to their house to see them?"

"What, now?"

"Yes."

"It's a bit late, isn't it?" I said.

"It's ok, they know you've just finished work. They said to come round only if you're not too tired."

"I'm not tired, I'd like to meet them." I said.

We went round to see them and I instantly liked them a lot. We were to become firm friends forever. They were from Liverpool originally and like me had moved to Barrow-in-Furness. Sharon's brother was over for a visit and Sharon and Patrick brought him round to our house to meet him. We decided to go out for a drink and on returning home, we found a note in out letter basket. (We had to have a letter basket because Ben had a hate for people pushing things through our letterbox and would angrily push them back through at them, therefore it was far easier to have a letter basket.) The note read: Glynis, your mum and dad rang us. Your grandad has just died. Love Mum and Dad E.

I stood staring at the note reflecting on my dear grandad with tears in my eyes. Darren looked concerned.

"What's up love?" he asked.

I held out the note to him and he read it. I couldn't speak with the lump in my throat, so he just cuddled me. There was nothing to say.

Darren, Sharon and Patrick wanted me to join in with the CB crowd.

"Go on, choose a handle," Darren coaxed me. "Then you can talk to people too."

Quite frankly the thought of making small talk to people I didn't know and couldn't see just didn't appeal to me. However I decided to humour them and we went to what was called an 'eyeball' which was a meeting with other CB users.

"Ok, I'll call myself 'Cockney Rebel'."

This was my nickname at work, due to my accent and my fiery nature.

"That one is taken," said the man in charge at the eyeball.

"Oh, ok then. Call me Hot Gossip," I stated boldly, and that stuck.

However I still didn't go on the CB much, simply because I had no inclination to do so, but Darren was obsessed with it. Whichever shift I happened to be on, whatever time it was, you can be sure Darren was talking to someone on the CB. That was fine, but it became apparent that there was one particular girl that Darren would be chatting to a great deal. It got that he was talking to her almost all the time.

"Why do you have to keep on talking to her?" I asked him angrily.

"Why not? She's just a CB mate," he replied.

I wasn't convinced and became extremely suspicious.

"You're just paranoid," he taunted.

But I would wake up in the night and he wouldn't be beside me, so I would cautiously creep downstairs to hear them talking yet again. When I would approach him, he would cover up and make out it was me being silly, and that it was perfectly normal to talk to another woman in the middle of the night while his wife was sleeping.

"BUT IT'S THE MIDDLE OF THE NIGHT!" I would shout. "AND YOU'RE STILL TALKING TO HER."

This ridiculous charade went on for quite a while and we continually argued over it. Then one day it came to a head.

"We're not getting on. I'm going to stay with my mum and dad for a while," Darren announced. At first I didn't think he was serious and tried to shrug it off, but the next day I was round at Darren's mum and dad's house. Mum was showing me how she had changed Darren's old bedroom round. I was evasive and couldn't concentrate.

"Are you alright love?" she asked.

At that point I broke down.

"I think Darren's gonna leave me," I cried. Darren's mum put her arms around me.

"Surely not," she said.

"Yes he's going to come and stay with you."

"Well he hasn't said anything."

"Hasn't he?" I felt quite relieved.

"No, happen he's changed his mind," she said

"Yes maybe. Don't say anything to him, Mum."

I felt as though I had betrayed him now.

"No of course I won't.

Saturday morning arrived and Darren came downstairs with his suitcase. I just looked at him as I came out of the kitchen. I had made breakfast.

"What you doing?" I asked shakily.

"I'm leaving," he said. "I told you I was."

"I didn't think you were serious," I pleaded.

"It's for the best. A spell apart will do us good. I'll be back," he said with conviction.

"Will you?" I looked at him hopefully.

"Yes, of course I will," he reassured me.

I heard the front door click shut and he was gone.

I couldn't cope. I took a bottle of wine from the cupboard. I felt alone. I WAS alone. I reached for another bottle. I didn't know what to do, so I just drank myself into oblivion to the sound of Blondie playing on the record player.

I was on night shift the following week and went in to work on the Monday night as usual. At first I said nothing as I was hoping Darren would come back to me. But my workmates noticed the spark had gone from me and started asking questions, so I ended up telling them what had happened.

"Come on, we'll go out for a drink," said Gloria.

"Ok then, why not?" I agreed.

It was almost Easter so a bunch of us went out. I had only been out with Darren ever since meeting him, so I quite enjoyed the new found freedom. I had been phoning Darren's mum's house constantly since he left, but he was always out and he never got back in touch back with me. Paranoid was what he had called me. REALLY? I was pretty sure he was with that girl. Anyway I was quite enjoying myself now and to hell with him I thought.

I hadn't told my mum and dad about the split as I didn't want to worry them; they were so far away. I continued phoning them as usual but steered the conversation away from Darren. I had my work and my two Great Danes, Ben and Zoe, and that was enough. Darren had left the car for me while he took his motor bike for transport. So I would take my two dogs for walks down to the beach. I slowly got my confidence back and was happy in my own company again.

About four weeks later Darren knocked on the front door.

"Can we talk?" he asked.

"What's to talk about?" I said stonily.

"This house is up for sale. I'll let you know when it's sold and we'll split everything equally."

I felt a little bitter now as it was painfully obvious that he was seeing her.

"The thing is, it's not that great staying with my parents. I get the impression that they'd prefer you to live with them."

I just stared at him blankly. Well there was no answer to that, was there?

"Can I come back?" he asked.

"No," I said without hesitation. Although it was Darren who had initiated the split, I felt now that I had moved on and it was final.

"Well, can I stay here in the spare bedroom till the house is sold then?"

"I s'pose so."

I couldn't really say no; after all the house was half his. So he moved back. The house sold shortly after that, and we both began our search for each of our respective houses. We had become friends while living under the same roof, and escorted each other to view various properties. Each of us chose our own future home and a decision had to be made regarding our two dogs. As we both wanted to keep them the fairest thing to do was to take one each. Darren took Ben and I took Zoe.

Moving day arrived. Darren's house wasn't quite available, so he and Ben were going to temporarily stay with his parents until it was ready. However Darren helped me to move into my house, and at the end of the day Zoe and I stood at our new front door and watched Darren and Ben walk down the road, and out of our lives.

CHAPTER 14

It was July 1983 and my decree absolute had just come through. My foreman at work asked me if I would change shifts onto yellow shift for one week to be trained on the mansize tissues department, in order to help them out now and again in the future. The trainer for that department on our shift was off on the sick and they needed someone trained on there right now. I said I would and went in on mornings on the yellow shift the following week.

Right at the start of the shift the machine went wrong and a fitter was called to fix it.

"That's a good start," my trainer Alison smiled.

The foreman of yellow shift came over to us.

"Would you like to sweep up along the gangway, please Glynis?" he said.

"Sure," I replied, and grabbed a broom and started sweeping.

I was deep in thought with my head down while working, when a cheery voice brought me out of my thoughts.

"You can sweep under my belt anytime you like."

I looked up into the bluest eyes I had ever seen. The young bloke was very good looking, with blond hair and a lean physique. He smiled at me as I tried to work out what the hell he meant. I just smiled back and carried on sweeping, so he walked away.

Later that day, Alison and I were up in the canteen on a break. I was engrossed in my book and Alison was reading a newspaper when the blue-eyed hunk came over to our table and started talking to Alison. I didn't pay much attention and carried on reading my book. After he left, Alison turned to me.

"Somehow I don't think it was me he came over to see."

"What d'you mean?" I said innocently.

"Well, let's put it this way. He didn't take his eyes off you, and he's never struck up a conversation with me before," she laughed.

"Who is he?" I asked.

"He's called Jack Cooke and he works in distribution," Alison replied.

That explained the comment about sweeping under his belt I thought.

Jack came and spoke to me often over the week, at first through Alison, but when she wasn't around, he would chat to me.

The week came to an end. My training on mansize was complete, and I would be returning to red shift on Monday. As I was about to clock off on the last day of yellow shift, I heard footsteps running up behind me and a familiar voice called out.

"Wait for me when you've clocked out. I'll be just one minute."

It was Jack. I waited for him by the door and he came hurrying up to me when he had clocked out. We chatted as we walked along to the car park. Suddenly Jack turned to me.

"Will you go out with me on Sunday night?"

"Yeah, ok then," I replied casually.

"I can't take you out tomorrow 'cos I work for a taxi firm in my spare time, and Saturday nights are a busy time."

"Oh! One job's not enough for you then?" I laughed.

"What can I say, I'm a workaholic," he smiled.

He pointed to the blue Cortina saloon with a taxi phone number printed along the side of it. "That's my taxi," he said.

We got into our own cars and I set off first. As I was driving along Park Road heading for home, I glanced in my rear view mirror and noticed Jack was following me. As I indicated to turn off into Dundas Street where I lived, Jack overtook me and waved goodbye. I waved back and then turned into my road.

The following day my friend Sharon was round at my house when I received a phone call from Darren's mum.

"Hello love. Darren's put his back out and is laid up in bed. Could you possibly come and take Ben out for a walk?"

"Yes of course I will, Mum. Sharon's here with me, we'll be straight round."

"Thanks love."

We took Zoe with us as I thought it would be nice for the two dogs to see each other again. It had only been two months since the moving day. I told Sharon all about Jack and our date for the following evening and while walking along Rawlinson Street on our way back to Darren's mum and dad's with the two dogs, Sharon suddenly stopped and pointed to Jack's taxi coming along the road.

"Is that him?" she asked.

"Yeah, that's him," I replied.

He hadn't seen us. He was concentrating on the road.

"I know him, he comes in the garage where I work for his petrol. He's a nice lad," she said cheerfully.

Later, when we were back at my house there was a knock on my front door. I went to open it.

"Hello. I thought I'd pop in to make sure it was still ok for tomorrow night," said Jack.

"Yeah, course it is. Come in, my friend's here," I replied.

When he saw Sharon he smiled.

"I know you, don't I? You work in the Strand garage."

"Yes," said Sharon. "And you'd better get a shave before tomorrow night. My mate doesn't like scruffy, unshaven men."

"Yes I will. Don't worry I'll look immaculate tomorrow," he said rubbing the stubble on his chin and laughing.

Our date went well. He was such a gentleman, holding doors

open for me and pulling chairs out for me to sit down. I have to say I was impressed.

Three weeks went by and we had been out together quite a lot, when one day I was working on the wrapping machine and I could hear the blokes on my department cheering and laughing. I turned to see what they were looking at. There was Jack walking across the factory floor with a pair of cuddly toy dogs and a gigantic card with the words I LOVE YOU on the front of it. He marched straight over to me, got down on one knee and handed the toys and card to me.

"Will you marry me?" He shouted to make himself heard over the noise of the machinery. Oh my gawd.

"For goodness sake get up," I said trying to pull him up onto his feet.

"Not till you agree to marry me," he persisted.

"Ok, I'll marry you. Now get up, people are looking."

I was mortified. Everyone was cheering and laughing, which Jack seemed to be oblivious to. I think it's safe to say, Jack certainly knew how to make a statement.

Shortly after that, Jack moved in with Zoe and me. He had been living with his mum and dad since his own marriage had split up a year ago. He had a daughter who was eighteen months old, but his estranged wife did not allow him access.

Jack decided to ask at work if he could have a transfer from yellow shift onto red shift. It made more sense for us to be on the same shift, then we only had to take one car to work each day and we would see a lot more of each other.

After a while I started to feel ill. I felt sick and I went off a lot of foods and drinks.

"You should see a doctor," said Jack.

"Oh it's probably a bug or something. It'll pass." I said, but it didn't. I continued to feel sick and lethargic. It didn't seem to be getting any better so I decided to take Jack's advice and went to see the doctor.

"Is it possible that you could be pregnant?" the doctor asked me.

I was astounded. I hadn't thought of that. How stupid am I?

"Yes, I s'pose I could be," I replied.

I went home in a daze. When I told Jack he couldn't have been more pleased, and later he sat down to list all the baby equipment that we would need.

Of course I had told Mum and Dad about Jack and they had been up to meet him. Unfortunately they were not impressed with him. So now I had to tell them about our impending baby arrival. To be honest I chickened out of telling them on the phone, I had a feeling that they wouldn't be as pleased as we were, so I wrote to them instead. I received no reply, so I guessed I was right in my assumption.

Jack was one of five siblings. The oldest was Daniel, he was married with children, and then there was Jules, who was a mechanic, Jack was the middle child, then there was his sister Mavis, who worked at Bowater Scotts in a different department to us, and the youngest was Richard who was in the Army. Jack's dad worked at Bowater Scotts too before he retired. The first time that I met Jack's mum was when she turned up on my doorstep to warn me about the debt that Jack was in, but he had already told me so it wasn't news to me. He said he was sorting it so I didn't worry.

At work a new girl started on our department. She had been working on the toilet roll department so she wasn't new to the company, but the firm had asked for people to transfer to the kitchen roll department where I worked, and she volunteered. I took to her straight away. Her name was Sapphire, and we were to become firm friends.

Jack was a smoker which didn't bother me in the slightest. Darren had been a smoker and so was my mum, so even though I had never smoked myself, smoking had practically always been part of my environment.

"I'm gonna give up smoking," Jack stated with definition one day.

"Oh, ok," I simply replied.

Although I had not been the one to suggest it, I was all for the idea. To be frank I had never really got this thing of shoving a little white stick in your mouth and setting fire to it. The whole ritual was absurd, and I had never seen the attraction.

"I mean it," he continued. "The money's better spent on the baby."

I was impressed. That was dedication in its finery.

"Right, well I can't really help you with it I'm afraid, but I know you can do it," I smiled, trying to encourage him.

He started off great but after a while he began to be a bit on edge.

I was six months pregnant, and had to attend an antenatal appointment. As the appointment was when we were both at work, I just popped out myself while Jack stayed at work. When I returned to work I went round to find Jack in distribution to give him an update. I couldn't find him on the factory floor and one of his workmates shouted across to me,"He's in the break booth."

These were little booths that we could go into to have a short break, when it wasn't worth going all the way up to the canteen.

"Oh, ok thanks," I shouted back, and went along to the booth he was pointing to.

Imagine my surprise when there he was sitting there with a lit cigarette in his hand. I stood there looking at him, I have to say a little disappointed but it wasn't the end of the world, after all it was his idea to give up not mine. He looked at me with a defiant look on his face. He did not look at all happy to see me, so I just turned around and walked away.

There was an eerie sense of hostility within the car going home that day. The combination of my pregnant hormones and Jack's slight lack of nicotine was indeed a lethal combination. After arriving home, I started busying myself with some chores while

Jack disappeared down the cellar. He had car parts down there that he worked on for various cars that his brother Jules had. Jack didn't want me going down there as he said it was a bit dangerous, I might trip over the parts.

I was upstairs putting ironing away when I heard Jack approaching on the landing. He appeared in the doorway and suddenly shouted wildly at me.

"If I wanna smoke, I'll smoke. I won't ask your permission," he spat out with venom.

I wouldn't have minded but I hadn't asked him to give up smoking and quite frankly I didn't care one way or the other whether he smoked or not. I can only assume that he was mad at himself for giving in. I just shrugged and carried on putting the ironing away in the wardrobes. This seemed to wind him up even more and he strode over, grabbed my arm and pulled me onto the landing. I was at the top of the stairs trying to cling on to him as he was trying to push me down the stairs, when I lost my balance and toppled over the edge. I managed to grab hold of the banister and stop myself from falling very far, and I hobbled down the rest of the stairs as I had hurt my leg in the fall. Jack followed me down and continued his anger. He lashed out and hit me round my head and I fell to the floor. I couldn't believe this was happening just over a silly cigarette. We had three doors in the lounge, all made of glass panels. Jack proceeded to kick all of the glass out of them. Zoe was walking around the room and I got myself onto my feet and guided her into the kitchen. Jack came out into the kitchen and grabbed me by my hair, hauling me back into the lounge.

"You don't leave till I say you can leave!" he shouted.

I was frightened now. I had never seen Jack like this before. He hit me again and I fell over again. He started kicking me in my head, my side and even my stomach.

"My baby!" I cried, as I tried to protect my tummy. He kicked me in the head again and everything went black.

I came round to the sound of frantic banging on the front door.

I slowly got myself onto my feet and went to open it. My head hurt, in fact I hurt all over. I opened the door. It was Sapphire. There was no sign of Jack anywhere.

"Oh my God," she said when she saw my bloodstained face.

She took hold of me and guided me inside. There was glass everywhere. Some of it was stuck to me.

"What the hell happened?" she asked anxiously.

"I've no idea," I replied evasively.

"You sit there," she said gently. "I'll clear this mess up."

I started to get up.

"I need to help you," I said.

"Oh no you don't. You stay there."

She gently sat me down again.

"I have to make sure Zoe is ok."

"She's fine. She's sitting over there," Sapphire said pointing over towards where Zoe was sitting. I felt dazed and a little sick. Sapphire made us a cup of tea and as we sat sipping it, she explained that Jack had arrived at her door and demanded that she got into the car. He had told her that I needed her immediately, and that was all he had said. He had driven like a maniac, dropped her outside our house and then just driven off.

Jack came home a little later. Sapphire was still with me and as he entered the lounge she verbally laid into him.

"You arsehole!" she shouted at him. "How dare you hit her. You could harm that baby. You piece of shit."

She was livid. I had never seen her so angry. Jack held his hands up.

"I know, I know. I'm all that and more. I don't know what happened. It's this smoking lark. I've tried to give up but I can't. I'm so sorry, love." He was looking at me. "Are you ok?"

"Of course she's not ok!" shouted Sapphire.

Jack sat down beside me and put his head in his hands.

"Please forgive me. It won't happen again," he mumbled. I could feel my baby's usual movement inside me and I knew everything was ok there.

"I'll drive you home, Sapphire," said Jack. "Then I'll make it up to Glynis. It won't happen again. I'm so sorry."

"Well you'd better make it up to her, you toe rag, and don't think I won't be checking." She wagged her finger at him with a thunderous look on her face. "And you'd better drive a lot slower this time, you rat," She warned him.

Everything seemed calm now and Jack took Sapphire home. He wasn't gone long and when he returned he ran a bath and told me to go and relax in it while he finished clearing up the glass and made the tea. Later he boarded up the doors where the glass was missing.

"I'll get some more glass to put in the doors," he said.

"Oh no you won't. I don't want any more glass. Just paint the boards," I replied bluntly.

Soon after that, I received a phone call from my auntie Sheila.

"You need to phone your mum and dad," she said.

"Why? What's wrong?" I felt worried.

"Just phone them, love," she persisted.

So I did. Mum sounded so pleased that I had phoned.

"We'll pop up to see you," she said.

I was thrilled. I really needed my dear mum and dad right now. I was almost seven months pregnant. We had a lovely few days. Dad took photographs of my huge tummy and we had quite a laugh.

Practically as soon as they went back to Kent, I started bleeding and Jack rushed me to Risedale maternity hospital in Abbey Road.

Jack held my hand all the way through my labour and at 05.30 on Monday 4th June 1984 my first beautiful daughter, Hayley, was born. Her weight was 5lb 4oz and she was two months premature, so she had to go into an incubator in the special care unit. She seemed ok, although she was born with a birthmark that looked like a black eye and she was very jaundiced. The nurse saw me looking at her anxiously.

"Have you had a bad knock or a fall dear? 'Cos that can cause a birthmark like that."

Well, I couldn't very well tell her what had happened, so I just mumbled, "I may have done."

No more was said about it.

A few days went by and I was missing Zoe, so Jack brought her up to Risedale to see me. I went to the entrance door outside and gave her a cuddle. She looked fine so I knew Jack was looking after her.

All babies lose a little weight at first and Hayley was no exception. She went down to 4lb 11oz and like all babies had to gain her weight back before she could be allowed home. Although Mum and Dad had only just gone back to Kent they returned again in order to see their new little granddaughter. They had gone back again by the time I came out of hospital, though. Jack came to fetch us in the car and we took our new baby home.

A little while later, Saffron and Juliette, along with Juliette's son David, came to see us for a visit. David enjoyed pushing Hayley along in her pram when we went for a walk out in the afternoon, then we took Saffron and Juliette for a night out to Manhattans club, while Jack's mum babysat the two children. It was lovely to see them all.

We decided to christen Hayley. The ceremony was at the church just round the corner. My nana came up for it and Darren's mum and dad came too. My good friends Sapphire and Gloria were godmothers along with Mavis, Jack's sister, and Jim, Jacks friend, was godfather. Jack's mum was there as well. Mum and Dad couldn't make it but we had a good day regardless.

During Nana's stay Jack became very bickery and quite nasty at times. I didn't know why at the time, but after Nana went home Jack announced that they were asking for voluntary redundancies at Bowater Scotts and that he was going to take it.

"Well, what will you do then? The redundancy money won't last long," I snapped at him.

This was not the brightest idea that Jack had ever come up with and quite frankly I was worried.

"I'm gonna start my own long distance delivery business," he said excitedly.

I just looked at him blankly. I couldn't believe the stupidity of the man.

"I've found a cab for sale for £200 which is my exact redundancy amount, and I can get a trailer on hire purchase. You can make loads doing these kind of deliveries."

He was so enthusiastic, but I wasn't at all sure. I would much rather he stayed at Bowater Scotts so we had a guaranteed income. His idea was simply too risky.

"It's not a good idea, Jack," I told him.

"Oh you would say that!" he shouted. "You've got me being spied on at work by all your friends. Well I'm not standing for it any longer. I'm getting out of Bowaters and that's that."

He was very angry, but so was I. It was unfair of him to risk our livelihood just for a whim, and I didn't have a clue what he was talking about anyway. My friends were certainly NOT spying on him. We argued for a while over it, then he went over to Hayley and started to pick her up.

"Well, I'm leaving and I'm taking my daughter with me," he said.

"Oh no you're not," I said and went over to take Hayley off of him, but he lashed out at me and caught me on the side of my head.

I staggered back a little then went to take her again. I was in front of him now and he threw one punch on my nose and I was out cold.

When I regained consciousness I was lying on the sofa, the white blouse I was wearing was completely red down the front. My head hurt and I slowly pulled myself up to a sitting position. I looked across at the pram where Hayley was lying and noticed the pram and Hayley were splattered in my blood. I looked around and saw the walls were all splattered too. Jack was on his hands and knees trying to scrub the blood out of the carpet. I tried to get up from the sofa and Jack rushed across to me.

"No don't get up, love. Just rest there."

"Hayley!" I said faintly.

"She's fine, she's sleeping at the moment. She'll probably wake up for a feed in a minute, but I'll do that. You stay there."

I put my hand up to my head and felt that my hair was soaking wet. I began to shiver. I felt so cold.

"Sorry, I put your head under the tap in the kitchen. I thought it would bring you round but it didn't."

He saw me shivering and took hold of my hands.

"D'you wanna have a bath?" he asked. "I'll run one for you."

I just nodded and he disappeared upstairs. Moments later he came back down and gently guided me upstairs. I felt a little better after my bath. I was still hurting all over, but at least I had cleaned all the blood off of me.

The next morning I looked in the mirror to discover that I had two black eyes and the side of my face was bruised. Oh no, how am I gonna go outside looking like this, I thought.

Jack did leave Bowater Scotts, and he spent his redundancy money on a cab as he planned. Then he organised a bank loan and bought a personalised 40ft trailer. I can't deny I was very worried as to whether this venture was going to work and it turned out that I was right, as shortly after the purchase, Jack crashed the vehicle on Abbey Road and wiped out three trees, two cars and a lamppost in the process. That, as they say, was that. We now had £25,000 worth of debt and no income. Fan bloody tastic.

Jack, always the optimist, then decided to start his own taxi firm.

"Can't you get a proper job?" I begged him. "If you want to work on the taxis, then at least get a job with a proper taxi firm."

"Why should I put up with bosses telling me what to do when I'm perfectly capable of running my own business?" he tried to rationalise.

"What, like last time?" I replied sarcastically. "That was a huge success wasn't it?"

"Yeah, but I've driven taxis for a long time. I know what I'm doing this time."

"I wonder," I muttered.

I knew I was never going to deter him. He had made up his mind and that was the end of it. At least this venture didn't cost much to get off the ground. Although we had sold Jack's car to raise some money, we still had my purple Cortina to use as a taxi. Jack bought two CB radios, one for him to use in the car and one for me to use. I was to be the radio operator apparently, although I wouldn't be using my Hot Gossip handle this time. I have to say, I was a little sceptical about it working, but this time it went ok and Jack was actually making money, not a lot, but enough to keep our heads above water.

Jack's divorce finally came through and we decided to get married now. We set the date for 23rd March 1985 and Mum and Dad travelled up for the wedding, as did my old school friend, Sophia, with her husband, Norris. It was a small wedding this time, with the ceremony being at the Register Office in Ramsden Square, where I became Mrs Cooke. Afterwards we had a small reception just along the road at Whispers club. Jack's parents were also there and Jules, his brother, was best man. Hayley of course stole the moment, dressed in white embroidery anglaise, with the dress standing out over mounds of petticoats, finishing off the outfit with a white cape. Mum and Dad bought her outfit and she looked stunning. Jack wore a black suit and I was dressed in a red skirt with a red and white patterned blouse pinched in at the waist with a stylish white belt, a white headband finished off the outfit. Mum was horrified when she saw my outfit.

"You can't wear that."

"Why not?" I asked her looking at my outfit.

Gloria had come with me to choose it and we thought it was

lovely.

"It's red," Mum stated. "You can't get married in red, if you do there will be blood spilt."

Well, it's too late to worry about that, I thought. Already BEEN there. But I didn't say anything. Dad had already made it clear that I should not be marrying Jack, and the worst thing was I knew he was right, but I had the ridiculous need to be able to say that I was married to Hayley's father.

Mum and Dad stayed at our house for a few days after the wedding. On our wedding night we stayed at The Victoria Park Hotel. Then the next day we went to London for a few days for our honeymoon. We called in to see Verity as she was unable to come to our wedding because she was recovering from an operation and had only just come out of hospital. It was lovely seeing her. I introduced her to Jack. At the time she smiled but she told me in later years, she did not like Jack at all.

So now I was Mrs Cooke. Although I had changed my name by deed poll a while back as I wanted to have the same name as my daughter, it was now official. We settled down to married life and continued with the taxi business. The CB radio wasn't ideal however and quite often I couldn't get Jack to answer.

"I was probably in a dip or something," Jack would say.

Funny I don't remember Darren ever having trouble contacting anyone when he was in the car, I thought.

Pretty soon it became apparent that there was a particular female in the picture. At first I didn't notice, after all this was a taxi firm, and every time she phoned I would innocently send Jack to pick her up. However it eventually became quite obvious when she would phone in a drunken state in the middle of the night, and against my wishes Jack would scramble out of bed and immediately go to her. What's more he would be gone for ages. We started to row constantly over it, and predictably I would end up black and blue in the process. Often he would pick me up and throw me across the room where I would bounce off the chairs.

My eyes were blackened more and more often. I went through cover up makeup like I was eating it. Leaving the house became a traumatic experience as I felt people glancing at me where the makeup didn't quite cover, so I stayed inside the house as much as I could. My friends were constantly on at me to get him out of my life, but stupidly I didn't listen.

Mum and Dad came up for a visit in the September. My face was clear of bruises at this time although I had a few bruises on my body, but they were not visible under my clothes so I didn't worry. While Jack was out the three of us were washing up the dishes in the kitchen. I felt quite relaxed in Mum and Dad's company and while laughing at something Dad said, my sleeve rode up slightly and Mum spotted a glimpse of a bruise on my arm. She suddenly pulled my sleeve up and revealed the severity of the injuries. My back was also covered in bruises.

"Oh no, what's he done to you?" Mum cried dismally.

Dad was furious.

"I told you he was no good," he said angrily.

He went to get his camera, always the policeman.

"I'm taking pictures of these injuries. We may need evidence in the future," he said.

"I think you should see the doctor," said Mum.

"No, that's not necessary," I protested.

I didn't want any more doctors giving me that sad, pathetic look.

"Your mum's right," said Dad. "Even if it's just to get it on record. You may need it later on."

They were insistent, so Mum and I ended up sitting in the doctor's waiting room while Dad remained at home with Hayley.

The doctor's words will remain in my head forever.

"You know, Glynis. You can keep on coming here, and I can keep on patching you up. But think about this. You've got a young daughter at home who, pretty soon will be toddling around. What if she annoys him? Will he lash out at her? And more to the point, can her little body withstand that kind of treatment?" That was it. It was suddenly clear what action I had to take for the sake of my little daughter.

Mum and I arrived home and Dad greeted us anxiously.

"Everything ok?" he asked.

"I'm gonna pack his things up, Dad. He doesn't know it yet, but he is most definitely leaving."

"Thank goodness you've seen sense," he said.

"I'm gonna phone Sharon and Patrick," I said. "We may have a bit of trouble with him. We'll probably need backup."

I have to say I was more than a little worried about this next step.

Sharon and Patrick came immediately and soon Jack arrived home. At first he just stood there looking at the bin bags I had put by the front door with everything he owned inside them. After all, I owned the house and all of the furniture in it, and I wasn't prepared to split it with him under the circumstances. I figured he didn't deserve anything. He looked at Sharon and Patrick, then my mum and dad, and finally at me with a sadness in his eyes. He knew he wasn't going to win this one.

"Is this what you really want?" he simply asked me.

I just nodded. I couldn't speak for the lump in my throat. This wasn't easy for me either. He then picked up his possessions and left, closing the door quietly behind him.

CHAPTER 15

If I thought life would be a lot calmer with Jack gone, I was very sadly mistaken. In fact it got worse. I went from having a husband to having a stalker, and it became very difficult for me to leave the house. Of course I did have to go out, to take Zoe for a walk, to do shopping, and pay bills... etc. But every time I stepped over my doorstep, you can be sure that Jack would appear. He would kerb crawl along the road in his car, and follow me wherever I went. Sometimes he would get out of his car and attack me, and sometimes he would just follow me. He was so unpredictable I never knew what he would do.

While I was at home, he would constantly phone me to let me know that he was watching me. Although I would sound confident when telling him to leave me alone, secretly I was quite unnerved. At first he had access to Hayley, taking her out for the day on Sundays and for two hours, 17.00–19.00 on Tuesdays and Thursdays. This arrangement seemed to work for a short while. Then one day something occurred in his life, unconnected to me, and the wild streak in his nature raised its ugly head again.

"You'd better make the most of Hayley this week, 'cos when I take her out on Sunday she won't be coming back," he threatened.

"What d'you mean?" I asked wearily.

"I mean, I'm gonna make sure we both die in a car crash. If I can't have her permanently then neither will you," he stated. He was clearly unhinged and it was up to me to take action. I didn't answer him, I just closed the door. I had no idea if he actually meant it. In all probability he didn't, but I wasn't taking any chances.

The next day, I sneaked out of the back door early with Hayley, and headed for my solicitors via the back streets, keeping out of sight the best way I could. I was more than a little shaken, and couldn't hide the desperation in my voice as I related back Jack's threat to my solicitor, ending with, "So there's no way I'm handing my daughter over to him on Sunday."

"It's ok, Glynis, there's no need for you to worry. You won't have to hand her over to him. It's game over for him."

I was worried that I didn't actually have any proof of his threat, but my solicitor assured me that it didn't matter: a child was involved.

"Oh, thank goodness."

I slumped back in the chair with relief.

Sunday arrived and Jack rang my doorbell. I was hiding upstairs with Hayley. He kept on ringing and knocking for quite a while and eventually he gave up and disappeared. As soon as the phone rang I knew who it would be on the other end.

"WHAT DO YOU THINK YOU'RE PLAYING AT? WHERE'S MY DAUGHTER?" he shouted angrily.

"You didn't seriously think I would be handing her over after that threat did you?" I said.

"You have to," he said.

"I don't HAVE to do anything, so naff off, arsehole."

My stomach was doing somersaults but I stuck to my guns. He slammed the phone down and it went quiet for a while. I settled down with Hayley stupidly thinking it was over. A short while later, the police arrived. I leapt up and shut the front window curtains as they were knocking on my front door. I picked Hayley up and sat rocking her, ignoring the racket that was going on outside. The letterbox clicked open and an unknown voice reached my ears.

"Can you please open the door Mrs Cooke. We need to speak to you."

I didn't know what to do. Ultimately I was a law abiding citizen, but there was no way I was going to hand my daughter over, so I had a dilemma. Did I answer the door? Or did I go against the police? I walked over to the window with Hayley in my arms and pulled the curtain back slightly to look out. There were several policemen standing outside with Jack. The one who had spoken came to the window immediately.

"Will you just allow ME in to talk to you?" He held his hand up as if in peace. "Just me, no one else," he said gently.

I considered the request carefully and then nodded. I opened the door slightly and the policeman stepped in. Once inside he got straight to the point.

"The thing is Mrs Cooke, your husband has a document to say he has access to his daughter on Sundays, and two short spells in the week. You seem to be preventing that."

"Yes, because he's threatened to kill her. I presume he failed to mention THAT bit to you?" I said angrily. "Now I don't know whether he meant it or not, but given his track record I ain't taking the chance. I've spoken to my solicitor and she's told me not to hand her over. So you do your worst, 'cos I'm not giving in," I stated boldly.

"Oh," he said as he took his hat off and sat down on the sofa.

He studied my defiant face for a moment, then attempted to tackle this issue.

"The problem is, Mrs Cooke, he has paperwork to say that he can have Hayley. Do you have anything from your solicitor to say that he can't?"

"Well, no. It's gonna go through soon. But it doesn't matter what I have, or haven't got. I'm telling you she's going nowhere."

I had attitude now and he knew it. So after a long discussion of getting absolutely nowhere, we finally compromised and I agreed to allow Jack into my house and see Hayley for one hour in my presence, after which he would have to leave. I wasn't at all happy about this arrangement, but clearly the situation had to be resolved somehow, and this seemed to be the only solution without me getting arrested.

So Jack came in and was promptly warned by the policeman to behave himself. He hadn't been behaving outside the house and had to be restrained at one point, so he was told to leave the moment the hour was up.

"We WILL be round to check that you've gone," the policeman told him.

Jack did behave himself and surprisingly, he left exactly an hour later.

My solicitor took the case to court and Jack was granted 'doorstep access', which meant he could come and visit Hayley, but he wasn't allowed to take her out of my sight. The stalking continued, however, and everywhere I went, like the proverbial sheep, you can be sure Jack would always turn up. It became eerie, as in the evenings he would phone me up from the phone box at the end of my road, freaking me out in the process, as he would tell me what I was watching on TV and even the exact times I went into the kitchen or upstairs. As my curtains were closed and no one could see in, it's safe to say I was well and truly spooked. How on earth was he spying on me? I even started searching the room for a hidden camera, it was absurd and of course I found nothing.

"HOW ARE YOU SEEING ME?" I shouted down the phone at him time and time again, but he would just laugh and hang up.

This went on for some time. Then one day he finally told me.

"If I stand on the roof of my car, I can see through the narrow strip above your curtains."

"You're kidding. You actually stand on the roof of your car?"

I couldn't believe the length he would go to just to spook me.

It was official. Jack was a loony.

I became so unhappy. Then Mum and Dad said they had some holiday owing and that they had decided to come up for a visit.

"We've got a week off, love. Dad's gonna decorate your lounge and get rid of all that bloodstained wallpaper. It'll cheer you up and make you feel better. You can choose the wallpaper and we will pay for it." My mum and dad were the best parents in the world, and that was a fact.

We had a great week and Mum and I went to choose some lovely wallpaper, while Dad got stuck into the work straight away. Darren's parents, Mary and Derek, came round to visit one evening to see Mum and Dad while they were up, and we all had a great laugh. I had stayed in touch with them all this time as my opinion that they were a wonderful couple had never altered, and I never wanted to break the bond that I had with them.

At the end of the week my lounge looked fantastic. Dad had done a brilliant job and they were right, I did feel so much better. It didn't stop the harassment from Jack, but at least Hayley, Zoe and I had a pleasant sanctuary now.

CHAPTER 16

Two years had gone by since my separation from Jack, and my divorce absolute had gone through.

Most afternoons my good friend Sharon would come to my house and we would sit and chat, while Hayley played. I had put up a Wendy house in my lounge and Hayley would enjoy playing in there. Every Saturday afternoon as well as Sharon, a few other friends would drop in for a chat too. Sapphire and Gloria would always call round and a few others now and again. It became known as our girls' afternoon. This meant that I was never lonely and I often gave thanks for having such wonderful friends.

One day I bumped into an old workmate, Silvia from Bowater Scotts. She told me that it was her daughter's birthday coming up, and she was having a party for her, so she invited Hayley to come along too. She lived just outside Barrow, in Newton, and as I didn't have any transport, her husband Tim came and picked Hayley and me up to take us to their house for the party. We had a very pleasant afternoon and Hayley really enjoyed herself. Shortly after the party Silvia phoned me up.

"We have a friend who is divorced. He's ever so nice. D'you fancy meeting him?"

"I dunno," I said. "Jack will probably be a nuisance."

But Silvia convinced me that it was a good idea, so I agreed to meet Tyrone, and the four of us went out for the evening while a friend of mine babysat Hayley. As I was leaving the house, Zoe stepped outside to follow me, and I took hold of her collar and guided her back inside.

"Why have you got a horse in your house?" was the first thing Tyrone Wood said to me, and I laughed.

He was dark haired and rugged-looking. Also, as I later discovered, he was extremely knowledgeable. I liked him a lot.

My friend Sharon had introduced me to a friend of hers. She was nineteen years old, the daughter of a Jehovah's Witness, and she offered to babysit for me. I had been out with Tyrone twice when one night as he drove me home and pulled up outside my house, suddenly the driver's side door was yanked open and Tyrone was hauled out of the car. This took us both by surprise and I got out of the car to see Jack and Tyrone knocking seven bells out of each other.

"Keep away from my wife," Jack snarled at Tyrone.

"She's not your wife anymore. She's going out with me now." Tyrone spat the words out at him.

"Oh for goodness sake grow up the pair of you," I said in disgust. "Jack naff off, I'm with Tyrone now and YOU are history."

I was not impressed with Jack's behaviour. However, Tyrone seemed to be able to look after himself as he was giving as much as he was getting from Jack, so I left them to it and went inside to my babysitter.

"Who the hell does he think he is?" said Tyrone when he came inside a few minutes later.

"He's Jack," I stated bluntly. "A law unto himself."

Anyway Tyrone managed to see him off, because we didn't have any more trouble with him after that.

I introduced Tyrone to Hayley and they took to each other straight away. A few weeks went by and Tyrone asked me to marry him. I said yes straight away. I phoned Mum and Dad to tell them the good news and they were very happy for me.

"Well we've got some good news for you too," said Mum excitedly, after I had told her about Tyrone.

"What is it?" I asked happily.

"We're moving back to Barrow," she replied. "To be with you."

They had been worried about me coping with Jack.

"Oh that's fantastic!"

Could things GET any better? I was thrilled. My beloved mum and dad were coming back.

"Dad's getting a transfer on the railway and I'm getting a transfer to Furness General Hospital in the CSSD Department," she went on to explain. "Is it ok if I come and stay with you for a while until I find a house for us to buy?"

"It's more than ok," I replied. "It's downright essential."

It didn't take long for Mum's transfer to Furness General Hospital to come through and she came to stay with me. Tyrone and I went to look at properties with Mum as she narrowed the selection down for Dad to look at. They finally chose a property in Newton Road, Dalton-in-Furness. Mum and Dad's house in Gillingham had sold straight away, so just after Christmas 1986 the move was made, and Dad was transferred to Barrow railway station.

Tyrone and I decided that he would move in with me, and I got to know his family. He had two younger brothers and a younger sister. Bradley was the youngest, and he worked in the shipyard, then his sister, Annette, who worked at Furness General Hospital, and then his other brother, Neville, who was married to Sherrie, and who also worked in the shipyard and had two children, Mark and Craig. Bradley and Annette were still living at home with their dad. They had sadly lost their mum a few years ago. Annette had a boyfriend, Colin, who lived opposite their house in Hawcoat.

Unfortunately, Tyrone and I didn't work out, and we split amicably a couple of months later.

CHAPTER 17

It was back to being my girls and I again, Hayley, Zoe and me. Hayley was three years old now and I enrolled her at the local nursery school. Hindpool nursery school was excellent and Hayley went happily along for the mornings of every week day.

Now that I was on my own once more Jack started becoming a problem again. One Sunday, Dad came down to fetch Hayley and me up to their house for Sunday dinner, when Jack, after seeing Hayley decided to be awkward.

"You're not going anywhere," he said, looking at me.

"Why?" I said wearily.

"'Cos I say so."

Dad, Hayley and I went back into my house again.

"I'll go and get the police, they'll shift him," said dad. So off he went, and I stayed inside waiting for him to bring the police. He arrived back with only one police officer, which was all that was available at the time. The officer had a word with him outside, but I could see Jack shaking his head, and I knew this was not going to be easy. The officer then came inside with Dad.

"Right. He's not going to co-operate, so what we will do is this. I'll go out there and restrain him, while you three get into your car and drive off. Ok?"

"Ok," said Dad.

So the officer went outside and stood beside Jack. He gestured for us to come out. Jack went to get into his car, so the officer grabbed him and tried to hold him back, but Jack got free and jumped into his car. What followed then was like something out of a car chase movie, as Jack tried to ram my dad's car off the road. Dad had no choice but to pull back over to the side of the road. The officer ran up to our car.

"I'm sorry, but he's not gonna let you go out of this road, and as I'm on my own there's not a lot I can do. Is it possible for you to stay inside for today?" he said.

"Yes, I s'pose I can go and get Mum down here for the day then," said Dad.

A little while later Mum and Dad arrived, complete with the pans of dinner that Mum had started cooking at their house, and annoyingly we had to stay put.

My good friend Sharon was still coming to spend most afternoons with us, and once every third Friday I went out for the evening with Sapphire, and sometimes Gloria came too. Mum and Dad would have Hayley overnight at their house. One evening Sapphire and I were sitting chatting in Manhattans, a local club, when a figure appeared in front of us. It was Bradley, Tyrone's younger brother. Bradley was tall, dark and handsome and kept himself extremely fit.

"Hello. How are you?" he said smiling at me.

"Fine, thanks. How are you?" I replied.

"Yeah I'm ok, thanks. I'm out on my mate's girlfriend's twenty-first birthday," he said, pointing across the room to where they were sitting.

It seemed like he wanted to chat, so I asked him to sit down, and he did. Bradley always seemed very shy whenever I had seen him at Tyrone's dad's house and I knew it couldn't have been easy for him to approach me, so I tried to make him feel at ease in our company. Eventually he asked me to dance and I asked Sapphire if she minded, as we were, after all, out together.

"No of course not," she assured me.

At the end of the evening Sapphire asked me if I wanted a lift home as usual. Sapphire's boyfriend, Shane, was extremely nice. He was very placid and took everything in his stride. I can honestly say that I had never seen Shane get annoyed at anything and he always made sure that we got home safely after our evenings out, whatever time we surfaced from the club. A truly wonderful bloke.

"I'll walk you home," Bradley volunteered.

"Are you sure? It's a bit out of your way," I said.

"Yeah, it's no problem," he replied.

"Ok. Thanks Sapphire but Bradley's gonna see me home."

"Right, well if you're sure," Sapphire said warily.

"Oh yes, Bradley's ok," I reassured her.

Normally I never allowed anyone to walk me home. I always went home with Sapphire and Shane, but this was different, I knew Bradley.

After our walk home, I made Bradley a cup of coffee. It was perfectly clear that Bradley was a gentleman and I felt comfortable with him. Even though he was younger than me, the age difference didn't seem to matter. On seeing Bradley out, he kissed me goodnight and asked if he could take me out tomorrow evening.

"Well I can't really, 'cos I don't like to ask my mum and dad to have Hayley too often. They have her once every three weeks and I like to stick to that. I could see that he was a little disappointed so I added, "But you could come round here for the evening if you like?"

He immediately smiled. "Yes ok, what time?"

"Anytime after seven. Hayley will be in bed by then," I replied.

We had a lovely evening, and many more lovely evenings after that. Bradley possessed a similar nature to Tyrone which was not altogether surprising as they were very close. However Bradley seemed to have all the nice qualities of Tyrone and then some. Mum and Dad liked him too, which was a bonus.

Jack had been cooperative for quite a while now continuing to come and see Hayley once a week on a Sunday morning, after which Hayley and I would spend the rest of the day at Mum and Dad's. Of course the inevitable happened and Jack spotted Bradley walking me home one night.

"I'm not having him taking over my daughter," he ranted.

The man was like an irritating wasp that just wouldn't buzz off, and I was fed up to the back teeth with him.

"Don't worry. I'll take Hayley to the door when he turns up next week. You don't have to deal with him anymore. I will," said Bradley when I told him about Jack's ranting and raving again.

True to his word, Bradley turned up the following Sunday and took Hayley to the door. Mum and Dad came round too and we listened to the conversation; that is to say, Jack's shouting and bawling and Bradley's calm, clever use of words. With Bradley being a body builder, Jack knew he wouldn't win if it came to a fight. So finally, my long drawn out war had been won. Jack never returned.

Life was good. It had been a long time since I had peace of mind without worrying about the next time Jack would kick off with his Jekyll and Hyde personality. I now had a good bloke in my life and Hayley loved him too. Hayley was a very placid child, and everyone adored her. I was extremely proud of my gorgeous daughter.

Christmas was just around the corner and Bradley kind of hinted about moving in with us. He was never pushy or forward so would never put me in the awkward position of turning him down, but after Tyrone I really didn't want to go down that road again. But at the same time I didn't want to lose Bradley or make him think that I didn't care about him, because I did. So a great deal of tact had to be applied here.

"I really don't think I should have another man living here, it's not fair on Hayley. She needs stability. I have to put her first," I told Bradley.

"Well there's only one thing for it isn't there?"

He looked at me smiling. For a minute there, I thought he was going to call it a day, until he added, "We'll have to get married."

Well it wasn't the most romantic of proposals, but never the less I was thrilled and it was definitely what I wanted. Before I could come out with my yes he held his hand up.

"No don't answer yet. I'll re phrase that another day."

That was Bradley, always the perfectionist. Well there was no answer to that was there. So I had to be content with the knowledge that it would happen.

It was New Year's Eve and we were out celebrating. Hayley was sleeping over at Mum and Dad's house. Midnight struck and Bradley got down on one knee.

"Will you marry me?" he said smiling, as the hour was striking twelve.

"Yes," I replied, laughing. A perfect end to a perfect evening.

CHAPTER 18

Our wedding day arrived. It was the 20th February 1988, a chilly but dry day. Hayley and my friends Delia and Martin's daughter Alice, who was the same age as Hayley, were my bridesmaids. Dressed in knee length royal blue velvet dresses, the two three-year-olds looked adorable. Bradley wore a grey suit and I was dressed in a fitted pale blue skirt suit. The jacket was pinched in at the waist and had a peplum style at the bottom, with a black satin blouse and a Princess Diana style black hat.

Bradley was waiting at the Register Office in Abbey Road next door to the Co-op Departmental Store when Dad and I arrived, followed by Mum with my two gorgeous bridesmaids. All of our family and friends were there. Sapphire was my witness and Bradley's friend Tyler was his best man. We had a wonderful day and only had a little way down the road to go to The Duke of Edinburgh hotel for our reception. Dad treated us to an evening do at the same place and a good time was had by all. I was now Mrs Wood. Mum and Dad took Hayley back to their house for the night and we stayed at the hotel. We didn't go away on honeymoon.

Tyrone had got married to a lovely girl, Estelle, not long before our wedding day, and Annette and Colin were getting married a little while after our wedding.

A short time passed and I started with that sickly feeling again. After a visit to the doctor it was confirmed that I was expecting my second child. We were all thrilled.

This pregnancy was significantly calmer, until around six weeks from the end. My beloved Zoe became ill. She wasn't eating much and she became unsteady on her legs. The vet was very sympathetic as he explained that Zoe was an old lady and very soon it may be coming to her time to go. But they gave me some tablets for her and told me to keep an eye on her. They said that I would know when it was time. I was extremely distressed. I couldn't face the fact that I may have to say farewell to my faithful friend. We had been together for nine years. Husbands had come and gone, but my beautiful Great Dane had been by my side through the good times and the bad. I was taken into hospital and put on a drip under protest, but I had no choice as my baby was distressed too. I couldn't bear to leave my Zoe but I knew Bradley would look after her, as well as Hayley. Even so, that thought didn't ease my pain. I returned home a week later, after my baby had settled down and spent a heartbreaking last week with my best friend. On the last morning it was clear that there was to be no tomorrow for my precious Zoe, and the time had come for me to say a heartfelt goodbye. I put my arms around her neck and whispered my eternal love for her. Bradley took my hand and tried to console me.

"I'll get Tyler to come round and take her in his car to make her as comfortable as possible, love."

I got up to get ready to go.

"You're not going," said Bradley.

"I've got to be with her. I owe her that," I sobbed.

"You know the doctor said that you must rest, for the baby's sake," he protested. "I will be with her right up until the end, I promise," he assured me.

The tears rolled uncontrollably down my face as I stood and watched Zoe be driven down the road, and out of my life forever.

It was exactly one month before my due date when my youngest daughter decided to make her appearance. This time I didn't have a natural birth as my baby was slightly distressed. So I was wheeled along to the operating theatre to have a Caesarean section, and at 7.45 on Tuesday 6th September 1988 our baby daughter was born. After coming round I went into shock and was wrapped in several blankets. I felt so cold and couldn't stop shivering.

"You have a little girl," I heard someone say.

"Where is she?" I mumbled drowsily.

"She's just getting weighed. She'll be with you in a minute," said the nurse who had spoken before. I fell in and out of consciousness and after a while became a little more alert as I realised that Bradley was standing beside my bed holding our new arrival.

There she was, our flame-haired little beauty weighing 6lb exactly. I felt so lucky. Although I didn't mind whether my baby turned out to be a girl or a boy, I secretly really wanted another girl as I myself had always longed for a sister when I was young. So imagine my happiness on discovering that I now had two little girls. I could visualise them playing together as they grew up.

Hayley had also been born with red hair, but hers had turned blonde when she reached three months old. However looking at our new baby I knew she would keep her flame coloured hair as she had eyelashes and eyebrows to match whereas Hayley had not. Deciding on her name became a debate, but eventually we agreed that we both liked the name Emma.

Later the same afternoon Bradley brought Hayley to the hospital to meet her new baby sister. She was clutching a medium sized yellow teddy bear.

"Hello darlin'. Come and meet your baby sister, Emma," I said to her as she walked up to my bed."

Bradley guided her over to the hospital cot where Emma was lying. Hayley studied her for a minute. She was four years old now and quite the little girl.

"I've got a teddy for her," she stated and held it up towards the cot.

"Oh, he's lovely darlin. We'll put him in the cot with Emma, shall we?" I smiled.

Hayley just nodded, not taking her eyes off Emma.

We had sold the house recently and bought a larger one in Cheltenham Street. Ever since I came to Barrow I had wanted a house in Cheltenham Street after I had viewed that one with Mum and Dad, and now here I was buying one. The house had been quite neglected but at least it had the third bedroom we needed for our little addition to the family. It also had a large run down garden. It was perfect for us though. So one month later, we moved into our new home and started giving the big old property some much needed TLC. The house needed a damp course and woodworm course as part of the terms of the mortgage, and we also had central heating installed. That was the limit of our funds for now; everything else would have to wait.

Hayley started at Victoria infants school as soon as we moved there, and I would take Emma in her pram to and fro escorting Hayley each day. One morning I found myself standing next to another mum whose daughter was in the same class as Hayley. She called out the name Heidi and a little red-haired girl came over to her. She also had a blonde-haired baby in a pushchair.

"We both have a blonde and a redhead it seems. What's your other daughter called?" I asked her.

"Her name is Shelley and she's not my daughter, she's my niece. I look after her while my sister is at work," she smiled.

After all the children had gone into school we walked down the road together. As we were enjoying our chat, I invited her in for a cup of tea. It was the beginning of a long friendship. Her name was Joanne and she and Heidi lived with Joanne's parents.

One day Bradley and I were walking along Abbey Road towards town. I was holding Hayley's hand and Bradley was pushing Emma along in her pram when a car pulled up beside us.

I froze. It was Jack.

Don't panic," said Bradley. "He won't do anything with me here."

Jack got out of his car and walked towards us. I braced myself for some of Jack's bad behaviour.

"I'm not gonna cause no trouble," he said holding up his hands. "I just wondered if you wanna change Hayley's surname to yours?"

I couldn't believe it. Why would he say that?

"What's the catch?" I asked warily.

"No catch. I can be nice sometimes yer know," he smiled.

"Ok then. Yes, I would," I said nodding.

"Right. Get your solicitor to send me the paperwork and I'll sign it."

With that he got back into his car and drove away.

The paperwork was drawn up and sent, and Hayley Cooke became Hayley Wood. Now we all had the same surname. Wonderful.

Shortly after that, we had Emma christened at the church up the road, and again my good friends Saphire and Gloria were godmothers, this time along with my good friend Sharon, and Bradley's good friend Tyler was godfather. Another great day.

Bradley's dad got a job in Germany, so he had to find homes for his two cats. As Bradley had picked out Kandie as a kitten it was a foregone conclusion that we would take Kandie, and my mum and dad said that they would have Pepsi, so that was them both homed, and we welcomed Kandie into our family. A gorgeous calico cat (more commonly called tortoiseshell-and-white), who I took to straight away.

Bradley came home from work one day announcing that there could be redundancies in his office. Bradley was an electrical draughtsman.

"They're taking on at Swan Hunters in Newcastle. It's more pay and I'd come home every weekend," he said.

I began to panic.

"You mean we're not going with you?"

I was devastated. He looked at my panic-stricken face and tried to reassure me.

"Well, not at first. I'll have to see how it goes. Make sure it's going to be permanent," he said.

It was logical thinking, but not to me. In my eyes it was another separation from the person I loved and I couldn't bear it. I was inconsolable, and convinced that once Bradley had gone away he wouldn't want to come back to me. I was very clingy and extremely hard work for him, but he persevered with convincing me that it was the best thing to do, and eventually I accepted that it was. I had no choice but to let him go.

The day arrived for Bradley to set off for Newcastle and I began to fall apart. My friend Diana, who I had worked with way back at Argo Jason, the sewing factory, was having a birthday party for her son who was the same age as Emma, and she invited us along. We were actually in hospital together having our babies; the two children were literally born two days apart.

"Come on, it'll be fine. He'll be back before you know it," Diana tried to reassure me as we were sitting watching the children playing in the church hall by her house.

I knew that she was right. I also knew Bradley was right to go, but I couldn't help the way I felt.

Bradley was starting at Swan Hunters along with two other blokes from his office and one of them had a car, so they were planning to all travel to and fro together sharing the cost of the petrol. They had arranged to share a rented house as well, but on arriving discovered that there was not a lot of bedding.

"I'll phone my auntie Sheila and uncle Eric, see if they can lend you some bedding," I told Bradley when he phoned me after arriving.

My aunt and uncle now lived in a flat in Gateshead where they were wardens for some elderly people living in the block. They assured me that it was absolutely no problem to lend Bradley the bedding and were pleased to help.

I concentrated on my daughters over the following week, and before we knew it Bradley was back. Hayley, aged six, and Emma, aged two, were waiting at the window, watching out for his arrival.

"HE'S HERE!" they both shouted in unison as soon as they saw him getting out of the car.

Bradley would spend some time with the girls before they went to bed, and it was around this time that he introduced me to takeaway pizza. Oh wow. What can I say. I had never tasted pizza before and it still remains my favourite food to this day.

Of course it wasn't ideal having to rely on Bradley's workmates for transport, as sometimes they wanted to stay in Newcastle for the weekend. So we decided to splash out and buy a car now that we were a little better off. We were able to purchase a saloon car this time as my much loved Great Danes were sadly not around any longer.

We carried on with this routine for one year, but eventually the whole arrangement became quite tedious. So when Bradley told me he had heard that there was a contracting agency wanting electrical draughtsmen to work in Plymouth, and that we could all move down there and be together again, well I wasn't totally opposed to the idea, although I hated the thought of moving away from Mum and Dad. Bradley had tried to get a job back in Barrow but was unable to. So a decision had to be made.

The contract was only for eighteen months so we decided to leave our house empty so that we could come back to it when the contract was finished, and rent a house in Plymouth. On the moving day Dad arrived to wave us off: Mum was at work. This was the first of only two occasions that I ever saw my beloved dad shed a tear as he sadly waved us goodbye.

"It's only for eighteen months, Dad, then we'll be back," I called out of the car window to him, and he just smiled a watery smile while waving.

I suddenly realised that I had a tear running down my own cheek as Bradley patted my hand in reassurance.

We had gone down to Plymouth two weeks before for a couple of days to sort out a house to rent. We found one in Warleigh Avenue, Keyham. Now we were heading for a boarding house along by The Hoe in Plymouth for the first night, as the removal firm were not delivering our furniture until the next morning. The boarding house was good enough to allow us to have Kandie in the room with us as well.

It was the 1st August 1991 when we moved to Plymouth. Hayley had just turned seven and Emma was almost three. We had all of the summer holidays to explore our new surroundings before Hayley started at Keyham College Road junior school in the September.

On Hayley's first morning at her new school I found myself standing in the classroom next to one of the other mothers. It was just like when Hayley started infant school when I had met Joanne, because this other mum had a red-haired girl starting school and a little blonde-haired girl around Emma's age standing next to her.

"Hello, is this your little girl's first day at this school?" she asked.

"Yes. We've moved down from Barrow-in-Furness," I replied.

"I thought I'd never seen you in the infant year," she said.

Her name was Cheryl and her daughters were Hazel and Stella. They were the same ages as Hayley and Emma. When the two older girls were settled in we made our way outside. There were two dogs tied to the school railings waiting patiently for their owner to appear, a greyhound and a lurcher, and Cheryl made her way over to them.

"Oh what gorgeous dogs!" I exclaimed.

Emma and I decided to go with Cheryl and Stella for a walk with her two dogs. It turned out that she lived just a few doors away from us and on reaching her house, she invited us in for a cup of tea. We chatted while the two younger girls played together.

Cheryl's husband, Ben, was in the Royal Navy so he was away

at sea quite a lot. During the day we saw a lot of each other, and while sitting in her lounge one day I asked her why she kept two empty fish tanks on high shelves in the alcoves. I presumed the fish had died and she hadn't got round to getting anymore.

"D'you think they're empty then?" she asked, smiling.

"Well yes, there's no water in them," I replied getting up to take a closer look at the tanks.

"You don't need water for what I keep in them," she said. I looked at her. I was intrigued now.

"What's in there then?" I asked.

"Spiders," she said.

I jumped back a step.

"Are you kidding?"

"No," she laughed. "I didn't mention it before, 'cos I thought it might freak you out."

I peered into the tanks to see a huge great black widow spider in one, and an even bigger hairy stripy tarantula in the other. I didn't know which one was the more scary.

"What's wrong with keeping fish like everyone else?" I asked, and Cheryl laughed.

Cheryl taught me all about greyhounds and their lives, and my heart went out to them. Emma and I continued to go for walks with her and Stella and her two lovely dogs after we had dropped the two older girls off at school each morning. I was seriously in danger of falling in love with these two delightful dogs and so in October, when Bradley asked me what I would like for my birthday which was coming up next month, I told him without hesitation, "A greyhound please."

"That's not quite what I expected you to say," he laughed. "We'll pay a visit to the dogs' home and see if they have one then."

The following Saturday the four of us went along to Plymouth Cats and Dogs' home. All the dogs were out in their large outdoor area. There were different sections, depending on the nature of each dog, and I searched through every section to find my future greyhound.

"I don't think they have any greyhounds," I said miserably.

There were lots of lovely dogs, but not a greyhound to be seen anywhere. I was so disappointed. I had set my heart on a greyhound. I decided to walk along the empty inside cages where they all slept, in case there was one that hadn't been put outside for some reason. The very last cage was labelled:

SALLY

BLACK GREYHOUND

I tore out of the building to find the others.

"There's a greyhound in here somewhere. There's a cage inside with her name on it. She's called Sally," I said happily.

I was so excited. We searched again and eventually tucked away in a far corner, we spotted her lying down.

"SALLY!" we all called out through the cage to try to coax her over to us.

At first she just looked at us not attempting to get up, but we persevered and she finally hauled herself up and limped over to us. Her fur was dull and she had a toe missing from one of her front feet. She clearly hadn't had her foot treated properly when the loss occurred, so one of her toes protruded further than the remaining ones, hence the limp. I went to find an attendant to get her out of the enclosure.

"We'd like to take Sally, the black greyhound, please," I told him

"You're kidding, there's a lot of fitter dogs than her here, you know." He seemed astounded that we wanted this particular dog.

"No, we definitely want Sally," I stated.

"Ok," he said, unlocking the enclosure door.

He slipped a lead on her and led her up the path towards the reception area and we followed him. "You just have to sign some paperwork, then she's all yours."

"Do you have any other pets?" asked the receptionist.

"Yes, we have a cat," I said

"Oh no. You can't have a greyhound if you have a cat. The two don't mix, I'm sorry," she said.

"It'll be fine. I've had dogs and cats all my life," I protested.

"I suppose it'll be ok in this instance, as this particular greyhound used to live with travellers and although they abandoned her leaving her tied to a fence, at least she had been used to living with a lot of other animals. So for that reason only, I'm going to let you take her. But if there is any doubt that she's not going to settle down with your cat, then bring her back straight away," she instructed.

"Oh, I can assure you, she won't be coming back. She's gonna fit in just fine, I know it." I told her.

The lady smiled and handed me the paperwork to sign. We made a donation to the home and led our new addition to the family to our car.

On arriving home, Sally spotted Kandie and immediately chased her upstairs. Kandie stopped at the top, turned around and swiped Sally right on her nose, letting out an enormous hiss. Sally backed off, returned downstairs and that was that. It was established who was the boss, and that they were going to be good friends.

CHAPTER 19

"We're moving to Dartmouth," announced Cheryl one day.

I have to say I was disappointed as I enjoyed Cheryl's company a lot. Our walks, afternoon chats and shopping trips were coming to an end. Every week I would drive us to Sainsbury's in Plymouth city centre to do our shopping. We spent a great deal of time together and I was going to miss her. On their moving day I cooked them a meal before they set off for Dartmouth, and we waved them off promising to keep in touch. We did visit each other for a while but eventually we lost touch.

Shortly after they moved away we received a letter from our letting agency saying that the owners of the house we were renting were returning having been away in the Navy, and they needed their house back. So we set out to find another house to rent. We found a lovely big house in Paisley Street, Stoke, that we wanted to rent and immediately made arrangements to move.

While Emma and I were waiting outside the school for Hayley one day, Cheryl's neighbour Sasha, approached us with her daughter Naomi. She was meeting her older daughter Serena. Her two girls were also the same ages as Hayley and Emma.

"Have you heard from Cheryl?" she asked.

"Yes, they're doing ok. They love it in Dartmouth. Ben is

teaching at the Officer's College," I replied.

We stood talking for a while and the next morning, while seeing our older daughters off at school, we chatted again. We must have been chatting for ages as suddenly we realised that we were the only four people still standing at the school gates, along with my Sally, of course.

"D'you fancy a cup of tea at my house?" I asked her.

"That would be lovely," she replied.

Sasha was very nice and the same routine I had with Cheryl seemed to be occurring again now. Sasha's husband Jacob was also in the Royal Navy and was away at sea quite a lot, and when he returned we all got together and became firm friends. We would often get together on a weekend and the four girls would play together. We found a local playgroup and took Emma and Naomi along to see it. They enjoyed themselves very much there, and so we took them regularly every weekday mornings, dropping them off after the older two girls went into school.

After a time Sasha discovered she was expecting her third child and eventually gave birth to a little boy. They called him Adrian. Sasha and Jacob asked Bradley and me to be Adrian's godparents and we were very honoured to have been asked.

The christening was to be held on Jacob's ship with the captain performing the ceremony. It was a wonderful day and we all enjoyed it. Jacob's time in the Navy had now been served and he got a job at Plymouth police station at Crownhill after that. From then on we all got together quite a lot.

Hayley had joined the Brownies and Emma was in Rainbows, but after my own experiences at school I was anxious to find some kind of self-defence classes for my girls. We heard about a Taekwondo Club called The Ki Tigers and we asked Hayley and Serena if they wanted to go along. They did, so we took them along to join. Serena gave it up after a while but Hayley carried on with it. After Hayley had been going to Taekwondo for a year Emma decided that she would like to join, and so she became the youngest member of the club. The instructor, Nick, named her Little Em which she hated. Every Tuesday and Thursday evenings for two hours, and every Saturday mornings, I would take my daughters to practise Taekwondo and I would sit and watch. They both took part in many competitions and displays. We travelled all over for them to take part and so consequently they won a number of medals and trophies. They practiced this art for four years and then decided that they had had enough. I was disappointed but ultimately it was their choice. At least they had done well and had formed an ability to defend themselves. Hayley had reached blue tag stage and Emma had reached green belt. It had already come in handy for Hayley as there was a rather unsavoury girl who tended to be a bit of a bully to Hayley. We told her to use her self-defence abilities and the girl was duly sorted out. Problem solved. They also went to swimming lessons and as there was also a swimming pool at Central Park where they went to Taekwondo we signed them up for a Friday evening.

I had spent half an hour with Hayley every evening ever since Hayley was very young teaching her to read, and later with Emma too. I spent a longer time with Hayley as she had learning difficulties and therefore picked things up much slower than Emma did. By now Hayley was eight years old and her reading was good. However, the same could not be said for her maths. I was never very good at maths but Bradley was excellent and he would patiently sit with her trying to teach her basic maths, but she just couldn't grasp it at all.

"Maybe we should think about getting a proper maths teacher for her," said Bradley one day.

He had spent hours trying to teach her but he wasn't getting anywhere.

"I'll look into it," I said.

It wasn't long before I found a lovely lady maths teacher who taught privately in the evenings. So on Monday's after tea I would drop Hayley off at her house and pick her up an hour later. This went on for one year until the school advised us to stop them, as they felt that it was confusing Hayley with having two different people teaching her the same thing. So we stopped the lessons.

Around this time we received some sad news: the death of my wonderful nana, Dad's mum. We all travelled to Kent to attend my nana's funeral. This was the second of the two occasions that I saw my dear dad shed a tear. During the service we all sat reflecting upon her life with fondness.

Nana was a Welsh girl and had never lost her lovely accent, despite moving to Kent when leaving school to work in London. She had a hard life but always held on to her sense of humour and high standards. Nana always boldly spoke her mind and passed this quality onto Dad and myself.

After the service we all went back to my other nana's house in Wellington Road and sat talking about the wonderful things my nana had achieved in her life, and laughing about all the antics she had got up to, when suddenly, a small picture, which had been hung on the wall for years, suddenly flung itself off of the wall, just like that. Perhaps Nana had ultimately had the last word... We'll never know, will we?

CHAPTER 20

The inevitable had happened, this being a place full of Navy people renting their houses out while away at sea, and the letter arrived saying the owner required his house back. So a search had to be made for a further property to rent.

Four years had gone by since we arrived in Plymouth. Bradley's original eighteen month contract had been extended and it seemed we were there for the foreseeable. We found a lovely upside down house in Shirburn Road, Eggbuckland. We all loved this unusual property built on a hill. From the outside it looked like a bungalow, but on entering the front door two doors and a staircase going down instead of up was visible. The first door led to the dining room which led to the small kitchen. The second door was for the lounge, complete with floor to ceiling windows which had the most magnificent views over Plymouth. Downstairs were three bedrooms and a bathroom. The quirky bit was the fact that the front garden was on the upstairs level while the back garden was downstairs. It was simply enchanting.

Again the move was very well timed. It was almost the summer holidays and Emma would be starting junior school in September, while Hayley would be starting senior school. Both schools were just around the corner so it all fell into place very nicely. Just for the last few weeks of the summer term I drove both girls back to Keyham each day, where Emma finished infant school and Hayley finished junior school.

Our weeks were pretty full after that. On Mondays Hayley had tennis lessons and Emma had tap dancing lessons. As each event was at opposite ends of Plymouth, I had to get the timing right of dropping off and picking up each of them. That was fun, contending with Plymouth teatime traffic. Tuesdays and Thursdays was of course Taekwondo, Fridays swimming and Saturday mornings Taekwondo again. We had Wednesdays free.

On Saturday afternoons Bradley played football for a little place called Beesands, so he would set off at lunchtime and the girls and I would relax. I taught them to play hopscotch and French skipping like Kate and I used to play when we were young. But unfortunately Hayley being quite accident prone would usually end up getting tangled up or falling over. Later, when Bradley got back from football we would all chill out in front of the TV and Bradley and I would have a glass or two of lager while the girls would have pop for a treat.

On Sundays we would all have a drive out and take Sally somewhere nice to run around. By this time her coat was gleaming and although she still had her bad foot, her limp had completely gone and she could run like the wind. It was such a pleasure to watch her. Sometimes we would go to Plymbridge woods or Central Park and sometimes we would get the ferry across to Cornwall and go to one of the beaches there. Sally loved water and would immediately lie down in any water she found.

Bradley suggested to me one day that as now both girls were older, I should get myself a part time job, as Bradley had quite a lot of sport going on in his life and sometimes I would feel a little left out. This would be good for me. I fancied retail work. I had worked in a variety of places – airport, hotel, sewing factory and paper mill – so remembering how I loved my Saturday job in the Co-op back in Watford, I thought maybe I could get a job in a supermarket. As I shopped in Sainsbury's in the Armada Centre I thought I would try there first. I got a job straight away. Just twelve hours a week which was perfect, 10.00–14.00 three days per week. So I could take Emma to school in the mornings and be there at 15.00 when she finished. It was quite a rush, as parking in Sainsbury's car park would cost me more than my weekly wage, so I had to use Park and Ride in Central Park, getting the bus into Plymouth city centre to Sainsbury's. This procedure only cost 50p which was good value. Finishing at 14.00, I would walk across the town centre and get the Park and Ride bus back to Central Park, then drive straight to Emma's school. It was a bit of a rush but I always got there ok.

While sitting watching the girls at Taekwondo one evening, I was chatting to one of the other mothers and we were talking about computers and how complicated they were.

"There's a computer course starting up at the school by Central Park. D'you fancy going with me?" she said.

"Yeah, why not," I replied. So we attended lessons once a week and at the end of the course I passed my first computer exam, Computer Literacy and Information Technology Stage 1.

Later, one of my neighbours told me about a word processing course during the afternoons at Hayley's school, Eggbuckland Community College. I went along with her and went on to pass four more exams.

On a visit to Barrow one time, we visited Bradley's brother Tyrone and his wife Estelle. They also had two daughters: Rozalind was two months older than Emma and Helen was fourteen months younger. Around the time Emma and Rosalind were born, Neville and Sherrie had a baby boy, Lewis, so there were three children all around the same age in the family.

"D'you fancy coming to Disney World in Florida for a holiday with us?" asked Tyrone.

Bradley and I just looked at each other, but after a long discussion the idea became very appealing.

It was 1994 and we were off to the USA. Mum and Auntie Ellen travelled down to Plymouth to stay at our house in order to look after Sally and Kandie for the fortnight. If I said that we had a fantastic time in the USA, it would be an understatement. It was a holiday of a lifetime. At least that's the way I felt anyway. Hayley and Emma loved it, although the heat was a little strong for Hayley as she was quite sick at first, but as long as we kept her cool she was fine. We visited all the Disney Parks and the whole experience was quite magical. If I had to choose a favourite place, it would most definitely be Universal Studios, but I loved it all and will treasure the memory always.

We had been on holidays to Haven Parks and they were great too. For five years we had gone to a different Haven site each time, and we all loved every one of them. They were the perfect holiday when you have children, and we could take the animals with us. We had a lot of fun.

Seven years had gone by since moving to Plymouth. We had rented our own house in Barrow out to tenants as the contract went on longer than expected. I had drawn up a tenancy agreement and had it looked over by an expert so that everything was correct, and had given this document to our tenants. However Bradley's contract at work was now coming to an end and as electrical draughtsmen were being taken on in BAE Systems back in Barrow, maybe it was time to consider moving back.

"Hello, Mum. Guess what? We're moving back to Barrow!"

"Oh my goodness, that's wonderful!"

Mum and Dad were both thrilled. We were all going to be in the same vicinity again. Fantastic. As much as I had enjoyed my time spent in Plymouth, it was nice to be going back to where, after all, I had spent a number of years.

We had to give our tenants in Cheltenham Street notice, so that they could find somewhere else to rent. They found another house fairly quickly and moved out. Bradley was offered a job straight away, so he went to stay with my mum and dad while I stayed in

Plymouth with Hayley and Emma to finish off the school term.

We decided to make some alterations to the house in Cheltenham Street before moving into it, so I arranged for builders, plasterers and joiners to do the necessary work from three hundred miles away, as Bradley was busy working. This wasn't an easy task and at times I was practically pulling my hair out, but eventually the work on the house was done and I got everything packed up in Plymouth. Bradley had travelled down for some weekends at which times he did the dismantling of furniture and things that I couldn't do.

It was time to say farewell to our good friends, Sasha and Jacob, and we promised to stay in touch.

CHAPTER 21

Term finished and our moving day arrived. It was August 1998 and we were back in Barrow-in-Furness. We arrived at the house to find the building work and plastering had been completed. The floors were very messy but that was easily sorted. We stayed at Mum and Dad's for a couple of nights until we got the house habitable and the furniture arranged in some sort of order.

Once we had moved into the house, slowly but surely the house became a home. We got the house double-glazed, decorated and carpeted. Bradley had designed and fitted a brand new kitchen and bathroom. He made a very good job of them and it all looked perfect. It was a long drawn out project but eventually everything was finished.

While we were still in Plymouth one of the teachers had very kindly looked into the best schools in Barrow for us. St Paul's was the best junior school and Thorncliffe came out tops for senior schools at that time. I managed to get Hayley and Emma into those schools for September.

The following February my precious Sally developed a tumour and she stayed overnight at the vet's while they did their best to make her better. But the next morning when I went to collect her I was greeted with the devastating news.

"I'm sorry, there's nothing we can do. It's kinder to let her go," said the vet gently.

He saw my face and tried to soften the blow.

"She's a very old lady and she's in pain. I know this is hard for you, but it really is the best thing you can do for her."

I had to make the terrible decision. As I looked at her, I knew this was going to be the last kindness that I could do for her. I held her tight and told her that I loved her, while the vet made her pain go away.

Dad had come with me to the vet's, and I was inconsolable as I drove home with misty eyes. I rang Bradley at work to tell him that she had gone.

"We'll all miss her," he said. "But you did the right thing in letting her go."

Hayley and Emma were both in tears when I broke the news to them after school. We were all devastated.

Three weeks went by and Bradley suggested getting another greyhound. At first I was apprehensive, but eventually I decided that I would like to give another greyhound a good home. Bradley, my dad, Hayley and I travelled up to Carlisle one day to the Greyhound Rescue Centre to pick out a greyhound to bring home, while Emma stayed with Mum. I walked along the enclosures where they were all barking.

"Look at the size of this one," said Dad from along the end of the row. I walked up to him and there, curled up on his bed and looking at us, was an enormous brindle greyhound. He didn't attempt to get up, he just sat there staring at us.

"Oh, isn't he gorgeous!" I cried. "That's the one I want."

This was inevitable. Show me a huge dog and I didn't need to look any further.

"You're not serious?" said the kennel man. "No one wants him 'cos he's too big. He won't get a home. Wait till he stands up, you'll see the size of him."

But I knew the size of him, I could see the length of his legs, even though they were curled up.

"Of course I'm serious. Can you please get him out of there, he's just got himself a home," I stated.

He got him out and put the lead on him that I had brought with me. We walked him along the track leading out, and he suddenly led me to our car parked on the side. He stopped at the back of the car as if he was waiting to get in.

"How did he know which car was ours?" I marvelled.

I couldn't believe he knew which car was ours out of all the cars parked along there. Dogs' sense of smell never ceases to amaze me. This dog had clearly claimed us as his new family, so there was no more to be said about it.

Rose, who ran the rescue centre told me that they called him Fred, but I decided to change to Danny. After handing over our £100 donation to the Greyhound Rescue Centre, we opened the back of our estate car that we had recently purchased, and Danny jumped in.

"Here's a muzzle. You'll need to use it on him until he gets used to your cat," said Rose.

"I don't think we'll need that, will we?" I said, thinking of Sally's first encounter with Kandie.

"Yes you will. This dog has come from the track. He's not domesticated as far as cats go. Take it as a precaution," she insisted.

Danny stood up in the back all the way home, leaning into every bend like he was riding a motor bike. He was hilarious. Once we got him home, we saw exactly what Rose had meant as he made straight for Kandie and tried to grab her. I suddenly realised that Rose was right, this was not going to be as easy as I had thought. There was no way this cat and dog could be put together for quite a while yet.

It was just a matter of time we told ourselves. If we were careful, we could train him. We put notices all over the house to remind ourselves not to let Danny near Kandie. Keeping Kandie in the bedroom during the day and Danny in the bedroom with us during the night, allowing Kandie to have the house then, well that worked. Well that is, for three days it worked. Then what happened next, I will continue to reproach myself for, forever.

One morning, as usual, I guided Danny downstairs by his collar. Kandie was a creature of habit and she never went out of the cat flap in the mornings until after I had fed her. She would always be in her bed when I came downstairs. That is, except this morning. Stupidly I didn't even look in her bed, I was that used to her being there. I just assumed she was there as always. This is a mistake I will always regret. I opened the back door and let Danny out for his morning wee as usual. I heard a cat's scream and it was all over. I phoned Rose and told her what had happened.

"Oh no. When d'you want to bring him back?" she asked

"No. I'm not bringing him back," I replied. "This was my mistake, not his. I'm not giving up on him, but I will be more careful with other animals in future," I assured her.

Danny's behaviour became a bit of a problem. After speaking to several dog experts it appeared that Danny had over-bonded with me. This dog would not let me out of his sight. I couldn't leave the house without him at all, not even to put the washing out. He had to come with me everywhere, otherwise he would have a panic attack. Everyone else in the family could come and go with no problems, but not me. This became a real problem.

We tried everything the experts suggested, including putting treats inside toys, buying a crate that he would have been used to sitting in at the track, anything to occupy him and make him feel safe but nothing worked. This was a big dog and could do a lot of damage while having his panic attack. Finally, someone suggested that we get a female greyhound for company for him, someone else to focus on other than me. I couldn't help thinking of Ben and how THAT didn't work with his destruction.

However, after speaking to Rose, it turned out that there was a perfect greyhound for Danny.

"They may be good for each other," Rose told me. "She's

extremely nervous and Danny might bring her out of herself, and at the same time she might calm Danny down."

We travelled to Dumfries to meet this timid dog. There she was, a black greyhound who looked just like Sally. She was hiding in the corner of the kennel not wanting to come out. I went over to her and coaxed her outside to meet Danny. The two dogs were such opposites I really didn't think this would work. However Rose certainly knew her greyhounds. Imagine my surprise when Danny took one sniff at her, and then the two dogs started leaping and bounding around the field together. What a wonderful sight. This was indeed the beginning of a close relationship between them. We paid our donation, opened the back of the car and they both jumped in immediately as if it was the most natural thing to do. Her name was Jenny and her racing papers came with her. She was an incredible racing dog and had won nearly every race she had been entered into. On the way home Bradley suggested calling her Pippa. I liked that a lot, so it stuck.

We would take them to the beach often and watch the wonderful sight of them racing around the beach together. Danny was slightly faster as he had longer legs, but Pippa was very agile so there really wasn't much in it. Of course the beach would have to be deserted, as we could not take any risks as far as other animals were concerned. One day Pippa actually snatched a seagull from the air as it was taking off. That is how dangerously fast these dogs were.

Two years went by when Hayley arrived home one day after walking home from town with our next door neighbour.

"You'll never guess what," she said excitedly coming down the hall and into the kitchen.

"No I can't. What?" I asked.

I was intrigued to know why she was so excited.

"Next door has got to find a home for one of their cats," she said.

"Which one?" I enquired.

"Marmaduke."

"No, she's my favourite!" I cried. Whenever our neighbours went away, I would go in and feed their four cats for them, and Marmaduke, a lovely calico cat who looked like Kandie was my favourite.

"Can we have her?" Hayley begged.

"I don't know, love. It's risky."

I certainly didn't want an action replay of what had happened to Kandie. I couldn't take another cat's death on my conscience.

"I'll phone Dad, see what he thinks."

"Well, we know what to expect this time. We'll be more careful," he said.

So I went next door and asked them if we could have Marmaduke. They said that we could. I decided that the name Marmaduke was too much of a mouthful to say, so I changed her name to Kim. They brought her round that evening and we put her into Danny's crate that wasn't used anymore. She was perfectly safe and Danny and Pippa circled the crate, while Kim proceeded to let them know exactly who was going to be boss here. She hissed and spat and lashed out at them with her claws out, her paw coming out between the bars without actually touching them, until they both backed off in submission.

Gradually over the course of around three months, with very careful, handling, bringing them closer and closer together slowly, they finally settled down together. However Kim was such a powerful presence that neither dog would hardly dare to even look at Kim as a warning swipe would directly follow any glance aimed in her direction.

We became confident enough to even the side up, and so on going along to the cat shelter, we picked out a lovely, quite large tabby-and-white tom cat to join our extending family. As I had chosen Kim's name, Bradley decided to name him Bob, which was ironic really as we soon discovered that this cat was an unscrupulous thief. He had a strange habit of collecting sponges.

Bob would go out and find or steal sponges of various shapes and sizes. He just didn't care whose garage he entered, in order to bring home any form of sponge he could get his paws on. He would then proceed to push, shove and tug them through our cat flap, dropping them victoriously at our feet. Hence we nicknamed him SpongeBob, after the cartoon character. This habit went on to become an obsession with him and he went on to collect other items as well. Gradually we accumulated different sized hats, gloves, socks and hair decorations. I was seriously considering placing a box outside our garden gate for our neighbours to claim back their stolen items.

Mum and Dad decided to move house, as the garden was getting a bit much to keep up, and the hill down into Dalton was a little steep for them. They were both retired now. Mum had retired due to her health at the age of fifty-six and Dad had now taken his last train out aged sixty-five. Dad had a party on his final train journey as a guard. Along with Mum and lots of friends, they decorated the train, and with plenty of food and drink a great time was had by all. We were still living in Plymouth at the time so we missed the train party due to work, but we travelled up for his proper retirement do at the British Legion, and had a wonderful, although sad, time, due to the fact that Dad was going to seriously miss the railway. Mum and Dad bought a house in Ainsley Street in Barrow, and along with a removal firm, we all helped them to settle in.

Hayley and Emma decided that they would like to have their own pets to look after. Hayley was mad about rats, while Emma preferred gerbils. So we bought two rats for Hayley and intended buying two gerbils for Emma; however on arriving at the shop, there were three gerbils left in the cage and we couldn't leave one behind, so Emma got the three of them. We also bought all of the equipment, and they looked after their pets themselves. Unfortunately however, Hayley's two female rats actually turned out to be one female and one male, consequently we ended up with ten rats. Triffic!

We couldn't possibly keep ten rats, so when the babies were old enough to leave Mum, Hayley had to say a tearful goodbye to six of them. She found them good homes and now Hayley was left with four rats.

Another holiday abroad was on the cards next. Tyrone, Bradley's brother had split up with his wife a while ago and had a new partner, Carol. She was very nice also, and so we all decided to go on holiday to Spain. We hired a villa with a swimming pool, and Tyrone and family hired an apartment on a luxury site. We all got together to go out to various places like Morocco and Gibraltar. While in Morocco, I had to rescue Hayley from a man trying to put her onto a camel, but apart from that we had two wonderful weeks, although this time on our second holiday abroad it was poor Emma that suffered, receiving a bite to her eye that was so painful we had to take her to the local doctor. However it cleared up and we all had a good holiday.

CHAPTER 22

The house was finished and it was now time for me to look for a job myself. I didn't find it so easy this time, so I put my name down with a few temping agencies. I was offered a temporary job at a young offenders' school for three weeks to clear some typing work. The job was ok but getting in and out of the secure building was quite a task. However I survived the three weeks and going back to my search, I applied for a job at a local bookies. I got the job, but walked out after three days upon discovering that the job entailed working for seven days a week with no holidays and no breaks. They had to be kidding.

My next job was wonderful. It was only a temporary job for six weeks, working on the front desk at the police station answering enquiries. However I ended up staying there for four months. It was such an interesting job and extremely varied. I loved every minute of it and will always be grateful for that opportunity. One particular police officer was highly amused when one day I marched into the parade room carrying a bird cage with a bird in it. Some kids had found the poor bird in its cage inside a dustbin and, not knowing what to do with it, had brought it into the police station.

"What on earth do I do with this bird?" I stated boldly to the few police officers who were working in the parade room at the time.

Apparently it was the confused look on my face that provided the entertainment, and after the laughter had died down, the police officer in question offered to take the unfortunate bird home with him as his wife looked after animals for a living. I later became very good friends with this lovely couple, as after I finished working at the police station I was introduced to Joe's wife, Shirley, and I started accompanying her on her dog walking rounds. We have been firm friends ever since.

Emma started at Thorncliffe and Hayley left school all in the same year. While I was preparing to walk Emma to school on her first day, she boldly stood in front of me.

"Are you mad? I'm not having my mum walk me to senior school, for goodness sake," she stated.

"But it's a new school, love. I want to make sure you're ok. After all, I walked Hayley to school on her first day at senior school."

"What's your point?"

"Ok, well if you're sure then. D'you know where to go when you get there?"

"My friends will be there. We'll find out together."

This was the first time that I wasn't going to see my daughter into a new school and I wasn't happy. "I'll be fine, Mum," she assured me.

Hayley had done very well on leaving school passing a number of exams. She had attended a college one day per week to study cookery and art over her final year. The school chose a few special needs children to go there and Hayley was one of them. So Hayley came away with a number of GCSEs, Certificates of Achievement and City and Guilds certificates. We were extremely proud of her. She decided that she wanted to work with animals and gained a place at Myerscough College in Preston to study all kinds of animals. Of course she was going to live in for the weekdays, so we drove her to Preston on the Sunday when she was due to start.

Settling her into her room at the college, I began to fret. I was leaving my eldest daughter for the first time and I was going to miss her. With her having special needs I worried about how she was going to cope, whether she would eat properly and just about everything really. After leaving her in her new room and getting into the car, I was in tears.

"She'll be fine," Bradley tried to reassure me. "It's what she wants to do, and they have to fly the nest sometime you know. She'll be home at weekends anyway."

"I know," I sobbed.

The trouble was I had hardly ever spent a night apart from either of my daughters and I just couldn't bear the thought that Hayley wouldn't be sleeping under our roof all week.

However I did get used to it, and I drove her to Preston and back again every week for the following two years until she completed her course. I had got together with my old friend Joanne on arriving back in Barrow and she sometimes came along with me to Preston when I took, or picked up, Hayley. Once or twice my dad or my mum came along with me. It was nice having the company while driving. Hayley really enjoyed college and after the two years had gone by she came home with all of her exams passed. The last trip was definitely the best, when Bradley and I went together to bring all the things that she had taken to the college back again, like her TV and video and her bedding... etc. There were no tears that day I can tell you.

Sadly, Hayley couldn't get employment working with animals despite all of her certificates. It seemed that employers were a little apprehensive about taking her on because of her epilepsy. We had discovered that she had epilepsy a short while ago when she had her first fit. Before that, she had only had absences, and we hadn't realised that they were a symptom of epilepsy.

Emma studied drama among her chosen subjects and a real talent for film work was discovered. She wrote and directed a film for her exam and over the course of a year she made the costumes and filmed her friends in this fantastic production, having a part in it herself as well. They went all over filming this production, even up to the lakes. We were treated to a premier evening in order to watch the end result. Emma had thought of everything, even putting adverts into it. The whole thing was very professional and nothing less than brilliant. We were extremely proud of her. Emma's cousin Helen and three other friends were in the film, and they went on to form a group. Emma played lead guitar and she wrote the songs. They called themselves 'The Raging Hormones.' They were very good and the highlight was getting to perform at The Forum 28. Emma left school with ten GCSEs and decided that she wanted to study media and film. She was particularly interested in directing. So she went on to get a place at sixth form college in order to study these subjects, while Hayley became a volunteer at a local charity shop.

Pippa had been part of our family for two years, when she started to cry a lot and act out of character. So I took her to the vet only to discover that she had bone cancer. It had come on suddenly and took hold of her very quickly. She was in a lot of pain and so the sad time had come round, when we had to do the only thing left that we could do for her. I left Danny with Mum, while Dad and I took Pippa on her last journey to the vet. Pippa was only six years old and I thought how unfair life was to give her this terrible illness and take her at such an early age. As I held her close for the last time, with tears in my eyes I told her that I loved her and the vet ended her short life.

A new supermarket was coming to Barrow. Morrisons were opening a brand new store down by the Strand. I thought I would apply and went along to The Forum 28 where the company were picking people to interview. They told me I would hear in due course if I was successful. Shortly afterwards I received a letter inviting me to an interview.

Meanwhile I was standing talking to Des, a neighbour across the road. He told me that Kwik Save in Dalton Road were looking for staff and he suggested I go along there and see the manager, so I did. Coincidently I was offered both jobs, so I had to choose. I weighed up the options, although the pay was slightly higher at Morrisons I was offered more hours at Kwik Save. The situation was neck and neck, but I chose Kwik Save as I fancied the small, family orientated shop as opposed to the larger store. It was a decision that I never regretted.

On my first day I discovered that all the staff members were lovely, but one in particular was to become a very dear friend. Daisy was a wonderful person and everyone loved her. After a while our manager, who turned out to be temporary, moved to another store and although I liked him, our new manager Simon proved to be the best manager that I had ever had the privilege to work for. On the day he started he immediately went to everyone, shook our hands and introduced himself which I thought was nice.

As head of our little family orientated shop, he watched over us all with compassion and dedication that was an absolute credit to him. Des, who had recommended the shop to me, joined our little family eventually. Des and his family were lovely. They had a son and a daughter, his wife Pat was a school teacher and his daughter Fran worked with us.

One day Mavis, Jack's sister, came into our shop.

"Hello," she said. "Did you know that my partner works here?"

"No! Who's your partner?" I replied.

"Sam, he's the cleaner."

"Oh yes, Sam is very nice," I told her.

One morning while talking to Sam, he told me that they would like to see Hayley, as Mavis hadn't seen her since she was a baby. He assured me that they were not in contact with Jack. I told him that I would speak to her and see what she said.

"Yes, I would like to see my aunt and uncle," said Hayley. So we arranged a meeting with them and they continued to see each other from then on. Hayley also met her other nana once, but sadly her nana died shortly after that.

My two beautiful daughters were all grown up now and inevitably the time had come for the dreaded moment when BOYS came into their lives. Yes, love was definitely in the air and Hayley brought her first boyfriend home.

"This is Neil," she announced. Neil was very nice and we liked him straight away. She met him at the charity shop where she worked and the two of them seemed very well suited.

It was Hayley's twenty-first birthday and we had booked a meal at The Roundhouse ,a local restaurant on Walney Island, for a large number of family and friends. Emma told us that there was a boy in her life whom she had met at a local club that she been going to for youngsters. He also went to her college. We told her that she should invite him along so that we could meet him.

"His name is Josh," said Emma.

Josh arrived with his friend, and at first I was a bit confused as to which one was the boyfriend.

"So, which one of you is Josh?" I asked as they stood a little awkwardly in our hallway.

"I am," said Josh with a big smile on his face.

"Well, I'm pleased to meet you," I said.

The evening went well, Hayley had a good twenty-first, and we decided that we liked Josh.

I received a phone call one day from Mum.

"I've got some bad news, love. Nana has died."

Even though it was expected, it's still a horrible sentence to hear. We had been down to Kent to see her recently and she didn't look too good at all. We all travelled down to attend her burial and to say a sad farewell to my wonderful nana. Sitting by her graveside, I reflected upon all the good times I'd had with her and all of my grandparents, and now they were all gone. Nana was an avid Baptist and the last time that we had seen her she kept on asking to be taken to her Lord. Now she was at peace with him.

As Hayley and Emma continued to court Neil and Josh, Bradley and I were becoming further and further apart. It was becoming clear that we wanted two different ways of life. I wanted us to be together at all times whereas Bradley preferred to be with his friends practising various hobbies and interests. He had taken up kayaking, and what with that, the gym and various other interests, there simply was no time left in his life for me.

I tried going to the gym with him, but that didn't work. I really couldn't be doing with all that huffing and puffing to be honest. Then I tried going to a bridge club with him, but I was unable to grasp this difficult card game and my lack of knowledge quite frankly just irritated him. He became distant and downright sulky, so eventually I gave in gracefully and asked him if a divorce was what he wanted.

"Yes," was his short and most definite answer.

CHAPTER 23

It was October 2005. The removal men packed everything that I was taking with me into the van. I had found a lovely little house in Buccleuch Court and had fallen in love with it. Bradley wanted to keep Bob so I just took Danny and Kim with me. Hayley and Emma had both decided to come with me.

Mum was with me as I put Danny on his lead, picked up Kim in her cat box and left the house by the back door. I reached the bottom of the garden and turned to take one last look at the house that I had adored for the last seventeen years. I nodded my goodbye to it with tears in my eyes, and then turned and walked away.

We met Hayley and Neil, and Emma and Josh on the way, and we all arrived together at our new home. The previous owners were still moving out, which was quite handy as they were able to show me how to read the water metre and operate the boiler to the central heating. Once the removal men had got everything in, we all stood looking at the chaos that surrounded us.

"Right, what needs doing first?" asked Josh.

"Well, as long as we get the beds up and made and the curtains up, the rest can wait till tomorrow," I said.

Josh got the beds and the curtains up, while Emma, Hayley

and Neil started sorting the girls' bedrooms out and Mum and I started sorting out downstairs. After a while Dad arrived and Mum brought out a bottle of bubbly to toast our new start. As we all raised a glass Mum handed me a gift.

"Here's a little house warming present to watch over you all and keep you safe," she said smiling.

"Thank you," I said. I unwrapped it to find a little white chest containing three glass angels and a lovely verse printed inside the lid. It was all too much and the tears stung my eyes as the reality kicked in that I was yet again, single.

While working in Kwik Save I had met a lovely old couple called Bart and Maisey. He would hand me his lottery slip and the cheeky gentleman would ask me for a kiss.

"I don't give all my customers kisses yer know, only you," I told him.

This was a statement that Bart recited to me many times over the numerous years I've had the privilege to know him.

"When are you gonna come and visit us?" Bart would always ask me.

So one day I did just that. They were extremely pleased to see me and so I continued my weekly visits from that day to this. I loved listening to their stories from childhood to adult, and have remained captivated by them ever since.

Emma's eighteenth birthday arrived. I had arranged to take Emma, Josh, Hayley and Neil along with our friends Joanne, Seb and Heidi to Lancaster for a meal at a Mexican steak house, which had been Emma's choice. Arriving in Lancaster by mini bus, we entered the restaurant. The meal was lovely and the atmosphere was full of laughter and fun. Afterwards we made our way around the various pubs and bars around Lancaster town centre. There I was, innocently walking through a pub full of people after coming out of the ladies, when the barmaid came running over to me with some urgency.

"Excuse me," she said, "but you've got your skirt tucked in your knickers."

My heart sank as I turned to look at the evidence.

"Oh my God, she's not with me," stated Emma with a horrified expression on her face.

I quickly pulled the offending skirt out of my knickers and tried to carry on as if nothing had happened, and the whole pub wasn't actually looking at me with obvious amused expressions. However apart from my exhibition the evening went very well, and Emma came of age gracefully, unlike her mother.

Daisy played darts for a pub in town called The Cross Keys. The darts team captain, Vera, was a close friend of Daisy's and would often come in to Kwik Save shopping and have a chat with her. One day Vera approached me while I was working on the kiosk.

"How d'you fancy joining our darts team?" she asked me smiling.

"Are you mad? I'm no good at playing darts," I replied.

"That doesn't matter. We're really short of players and we're giving games away. I'd rather lose games than give them away," she said.

"I don't know. I'm more likely to do someone an injury that hit the dartboard," I told her.

"You'll be fine," she laughed. "Just come along and have a go. If you don't like it you don't have to come again."

"Ok I will, but I recommend that you all wear crash helmets."

I was thinking that she was probably going to regret her invitation. I went along with Daisy that evening and I really enjoyed myself with this lovely bunch of darts players. They made me feel so welcome. I never did ask Vera if she regretted her invitation, but I knew that I certainly didn't and I continued to enjoy playing darts from that day to this. I now had a hobby.

One quiet afternoon in Kwik Save Daisy and I were standing talking, when a tall man went through her checkout. Daisy watched him walk out of the door.

"Oh, isn't he lovely?" she said.

I looked up to see him just going out.

"Not my cup of tea," I stated "But d'you know who I think is lovely?

"No," she said. "Who?"

"That Irish bloke that you talk to sometimes," I said.

"Oh, I know who you mean. Yes he used to play darts for the Derby."

"Oh, well I think he's gorgeous," I said dreamily.

"I'll ask him if he wants to join our darts team," she suddenly decided.

My face lit up.

"Oh would you? That would be great," I said.

Daisy did ask him but he told her that he had his daughter on Mondays which was when we played darts. So that was that. But I continued to admire him every time he came into our shop. As soon as I heard that lovely Irish accent and looked up into that gorgeous face, I would suddenly lose all control of my legs and go weak at the knees. Of course all my work colleagues knew about this admiration and the moment he was spotted in the shop, would come round to the kiosk to watch my face slightly resembling a beetroot.

"When I win the lottery I'll take you away on holiday, so I will," he would say to me. Never have I wished for anyone to win that lottery as much as I did him. I wondered what his name was. He knew mine as the badge on my sweatshirt was a bit of a giveaway, but I didn't know his name, so I asked Daisy.

"I think it's Michael, but I'm not sure," she said. So next time he came in for his lottery I plucked up the courage to ask him.

"Is your name Michael?" I asked.

"No, it's John," he said smiling at me and making my legs turn to jelly again. "John Gillespie."

Later, I related the conversation back to Daisy, "Well I felt such a fool," I said.

"Well at least you know his name now," she laughed.

The deliveries to Kwik Save were getting fewer and fewer and the shelves were looking slightly bare, so John didn't come in very often. On the odd occasion that he did come in the shop I would relate it all back to Emma and Josh and Hayley and Neil when I got home.

"Irish John came in today," I would say.

"Terrific, we are so pleased for you," they would laugh. I think it's safe to say I drove them quite mad, but they put up with me with good humour.

Josh had moved in with us now, as he was at our house most of the time anyway it seemed silly to pay for a bedsit that he hardly ever used. So I said he could move in with us. Neil was still living with his family up until now, but Hayley and Neil decided to move into a flat of their own, and so our house went from four occupants to three again. We all helped Hayley and Neil with getting furniture and various household items, and eventually they settled into their little flat.

It was March and a man came into Kwik Save and bought a lottery ticket from me. I noticed he was hovering around the kiosk and as soon as I didn't have any customers he started talking to me. Some of his chat didn't make much sense to me, but I just smiled and eventually he left. I didn't give much thought to this fellow but later that evening while sitting in The Cross Keys on our darts night, he walked into the pub. He came over to chat to me again. He told me all about his life in the Army and I have to say he seemed quite interesting at the time. However at the end of the evening when he asked me if he could walk me home, I gave him my answer and left him in no doubt that I was going home alone.

The next day he came into Kwik Save again, handed me a note and promptly left. To be honest I found this to be incredibly odd behaviour. It felt a bit like playground methods, but I figured maybe he was a bit shy. The note told me that his name was Pierce and that he would like to go out with me. He had added his phone number for me to text him if I was interested. I stood there looking at this rather absurd letter and I strongly felt the urge to laugh. But

I shoved it into my pocket and carried on working.

Later that evening Hayley and Neil, and Emma and Josh and I were round at my friends Joanne and Seb's flat along with Heidi. After discussing the whole episode with them, they thought maybe I should give him a chance. The trouble was I still liked Irish John.

A few days later, we had a Kwik Save get-together in The Railway pub. Unfortunately Des was leaving and we were all having a farewell drink with him. My workmates knew about Pierce and my dilemma and brought the subject up again.

"So why won't you go out with him?" asked my manager Simon.

"Well, he's no Irish John is he?" I replied.

"Who the heck is Irish John?" asked Simon.

"Who the...? Are you mad? You must know Irish John. He's the most gorgeous bloke to ever walk into Kwik Save," I said.

"No. I still can't place him," said Simon, scratching his head and smiling.

"Oh, she's infatuated with him," said Daisy.

Later, round at Joanne's again, I decided to give Pierce a text after all, and we arranged to go out for a drink. He seemed ok and had certainly had a lot of important jobs during his life. I found him quite interesting, however after only one week he suddenly asked me to marry him.

"What! Don't be stupid," I told him in no uncertain terms. "I've only known you a week."

"Well I just know you're the one for me," he stated.

"Leave it out. You're a nutcase."

And with that, I swanned off. I continued seeing him though and after a while he kind of grew on me so eventually I agreed to marry him. This was a mistake that I realised I'd made shortly afterwards, when some of the things he had told me just didn't ring true. Slowly but surely I began to discover that the one thing that he was an expert at was lying. The more lies I uncovered the more bad tempered he got, and scarily I started to feel a bit like I was living with Jack again. He was getting downright nasty. Only this time I discovered that Pierce was a gambler too. I suddenly felt very nervous.

Emma and Josh had recently moved into their own house, and so that just left me, Danny and Kim now. One day my dad called round to see me on his way back from town.

"I'm not sure of him, Dad."

"Well if you're not sure, then don't marry him. Goodness knows you've had enough disasters already. You don't need any more."

I felt bad, but I needed my dad to tell me what I should do, and that was it. He had. Later, when Pierce was stood in my lounge, I told him that it was over.

"No, it's not. I will TELL you when it's over, and it's not," he shouted at me.

I began to feel a little uneasy. He pushed me, and I fell backwards into the chair. Then he leaned over me and whacked me round my face. It was at this moment that I knew I was doing the right thing in breaking up with him. He started pacing the floor like a caged animal, and after a while he produced a Stanley knife from his pocket and started waving it around in front of me. It was only at that moment that a slight fear enveloped me and I sat very still while I thought about my options. I knew that I wasn't going to be able to run, because he would undoubtedly stop me. I realised that my phone was close by and I managed to grab it and put it down the side of my chair without him noticing. In between his pacing I managed to type out the work HELP on a message and send it to Josh's phone. Then I quietly waited.

It wasn't long before Emma and Josh arrived, and as they burst through the front door, Pierce ran upstairs.

"What's happened?" asked Emma, as she was getting her breath back from running. I told them that I had ended it with Pierce and that he had produced a knife.

"Well we're not leaving till HE does," said Josh. We waited a short while and then Pierce came slowly down the stairs carrying a suitcase. He gave us all a dark stare and then left. Josh changed the locks on the front door so that I would feel safe, and we never saw him again. However I did in fact hear from him. Shortly after the separation I began to get a few texts threatening to 'GET ME'. How mature. The whole process became irritating rather than scary, but I still had to get the police to warn him off. Eventually he stopped and that was the end of it.

We had bought both Hayley and Emma dolls' houses a few years ago. Not toy ones, but collectors dolls houses. My mum owned dolls' houses and my girls had admired them, so we had bought the kits and Bradley had made a very good job of building and decorating them. However they had soon lost interest and had not bothered with them very much. So when both girls moved out of my house, they both told me that they didn't want to take the dolls houses with them. As I was on my own, I started collecting furniture for them both and making little things like curtains and bedding to keep me occupied. This became my other hobby.

It was that dreaded time again, when I had to confront the realisation of losing my beloved pet. Danny's legs were giving way and after several trips to the vet and numerous treatments, it came to the point where he couldn't get up. The morning had sadly arrived when I had to do the only thing left that I could do for him. I phoned Emma and Josh.

"I'm going to phone a taxi to take us to the vets," I sobbed.

I had left our silver Vauxhall Vectra estate car with Bradley when I left, as I couldn't afford to run it on my wage and also, living in the town centre, I no longer needed it.

"Don't worry, I'll ask my mum if she'll take us in her car," said Josh.

She pulled up in her 4 X 4 and Josh carried Danny out of the house and placed him gently on the back seat. On arriving at the surgery, Josh carried him in and lay him down carefully on a rug that the vet had put down for him. We all gathered around him, and after the vet had given him an injection, I held him tight and told him that I loved him as he closed his eyes and went to sleep.

CHAPTER 24

The occupants of my household were diminishing. We were now down to just Kim and myself. Hayley and Neil owned two cats Elvis and Derek, and Emma and Josh owned a cat called Lottie. They had recently gained another cat. However Lottie hadn't taken to kindly to another cat being brought in and promptly made her objections known.

"I don't know what to do with them, Mum. Lottie keeps on attacking her," said Emma.

"Well, bring her round to me. I'll see if Kim will accept her. She can come and live with us," I told her. Emma and Josh brought her round. She was a gorgeous little tabby cat, and she slowly walked around the room. Kim went up to her, hissed at her once and that was that. They were fine.

"There you are, it looks like she's staying here," I stated. "I think I will call her Holly."

The next day was Monday. It was darts night, and as Daisy and I walked into The Cross Keys my stomach did a flip as I looked up to see Irish John sitting there having a drink with his friends.

"Well, God's smiling on you tonight," said Daisy. We went up to the bar and I turned around to see Irish John looking at me. He patted the seat next to him and gestured for me to come over and sit by him. We sat talking all evening in between playing darts, and he explained that as he didn't have his daughter this evening he thought that he would come here for a drink. I was elated by his decision. He told me that he was a retired submariner and that he had five children.

"Five?" I gulped. "I guess you're not a big TV watcher," I laughed.

We got along great right from the start, and at the end of the evening when he asked me if he could walk me home, I broke my rule with no hesitation.

After walking me home and meeting my two cats, he asked me to go to the cinema with him the following evening to see 'Hot Fuzz'. I quickly accepted the invitation and as he kissed me goodnight and left, I was counting my blessings and considered myself the luckiest person alive. I was finally going out with my gorgeous Irish hunk. The following morning I excitedly phoned my two daughters.

"I've got a date tonight. Guess who with?"

"Dunno."

"Only Irish John," I stated boldly.

"Oh thank goodness for that. It's about time," they both said.

We didn't actually get to the cinema. We just sat in The Cross Keys pub and got to know each other.

It turned out that he also had a cat. He was called George and apparently he was large to the extreme. Now I couldn't wait to meet this magnificent cat, and after having been going out together for a number of months I urged John to bring him over to meet Kim and Holly, so that we could all become one happy family.

"That's impossible," he stated. "George will go for them as soon as he walks through the door so he will."

John clearly didn't know Kim.

"Don't underestimate Kim." I told him. "This cat has trained greyhounds that have come straight from the track. George will be a piece of cake to her."

John still wasn't convinced, but he arrived carrying the biggest cat box that I had ever seen, and out walked this extremely large, half striped, half spotted, bold as brass cat. He shimmied around the room taking in every element of his surroundings, when along came Kim. She waltzed up to him and looking up into his face, promptly hissed very loudly. She was half the size of him but had absolutely no fear. George backed away from her slowly. The boss of this house had been established and it definitely was not George.

It was September 2007 and two of John's children travelled down from Scotland with their stepdad to visit us. John hadn't seen them for quite a while so the reunion was quite emotional. I took to these two shy teenagers straight away and we all had a wonderful time, until it was time for them to go home to Scotland again.

Kwik Save was going down. It was near the final stages of its life and our manager Simon did a marvellous job of keeping us afloat for as long as he possibly could. A fantastic boss, but sadly, the day arrived when the shutters came down for the last time. It was my day off, and Tom, one of our under managers text me to tell me that our battle to stay open had now been lost. We were officially closed. I was out shopping with Mum and John when I received the text and we all went along to Kwik Save. Simon, and Jessica our supervisor were there finishing off paperwork and securing the building.

"We're finished," said Simon sadly.

All my time was spent applying for jobs after that. We received redundancy money, but that was not going to last long. I applied for everything I could, and finally got a job working at a local hotel. After the experience I had with the last hotel I worked for, you would think I'd give hotel work a wide birth, wouldn't you? Well, what can I say. I was either a glutton for punishment, or just desperate for a job. I'm not sure which, but I took the job anyway.

The job was advertised as 'hotel receptionist' which I have to say was a little misleading as it actually turned out to be a general dogsbody situation. This kind of thing was like a red rag to a bull to me, and so suffice it to say that after three weeks I was told very politely by the owner of the hotel that this job really wasn't for me. I can't tell you how relieved I was to hear those words, and I promptly LEFT THE BUILDING.

Maybe I should try Morrisons again, I thought. After all, they offered me a job once, maybe they would again. Quite a few people from Kwik Save were employed there already, including Tom our under manager. He had got a supervisor's position on the health and beauty department. So I text him to see if there were any vacancies.

"Well, I'll get April to print off an online application form for you. Then you can take it into Morrisons," he text back.

April was Tom's girlfriend.

"Put me down as a reference," he added.

"Thanks Tom," I replied.

I did put him down as a reference and I got offered a job. I was given the choice of checkouts or kiosk. I made the huge mistake of choosing the kiosk as I had worked permanently on the kiosk at Kwik Save and loved it. However this one was an entirely different ball game. It simply did not work, and was a total nightmare. My work colleagues were wonderful, however, which made the job that much bearable and we all muddled along just fine.

One month went by and it was my 50th birthday. John handed me a tiny box.

"Happy birthday, darlin," he said, and with that he turned to go and make us a cup of coffee.

Well. What on earth do I make of that? Has he bought me a tasteful pair of earrings? Or, is it possibly what I had hoped for: an engagement ring. No, it can't be, as the appropriate words did not accompany it. I slowly opened the box with anticipation. It was a ring. My heart was pounding as I slowly took the beautiful ring out of the box. It was my birthstone, a blue topaz, with three smaller diamonds either side of it, all set in a band of white gold. He later told me that he and his youngest daughter had chosen it together. I have to say a finer choice could not have been made.

My problem was, what do I say after thank you? If I say 'yes I will marry you', when there was simply no question, he might turn round and say that it's just a dress ring. Then I would want the floor to open up. But on the other hand if I say 'that's a lovely dress ring' he may have intended it to be an engagement ring, but think that I wanted it to be a dress ring. OH NO, I DON'T KNOW WHAT TO SAY.

After a lot of thought, I decided to put the ball in his court.

"Is this what I think it is?" I asked.

"Yes," he smiled.

Still not giving anything away. I still wasn't clear. This was hard work so I decided to jump in with both feet, and if I was left with egg on my face, well so be it.

"So. Does this mean that we are engaged?"

"Yes," he laughed.

Well. I have to say as proposals go, that had to be the worst proposal in history, but I didn't care. I was going to marry the man of my dreams and I was on top of the world.

Our first Christmas together arrived. It was time to put the decorations up.

"I wouldn't advise putting decorations up with George around. He'll just knock them down, so he will," said John. "I've never been able to keep a tree up since I've had him."

Well he's gonna have to get used to it," I stated. "Because the tree and decorations, are most definitely going up."

"Well, don't say I didn't warn you," he said shaking his head. I was quite prepared to fight George for my decorations; however there was no need, he quite happily spent almost the whole of Christmas curled up right underneath the tree, viewing us all from beneath the branches and not allowing the other two cats to come anywhere near it. It was perfectly clear that this tree belonged to George. We decided that John's problem with him in the past, was that he just didn't have a big enough tree for George to fit under. Now sitting under my six foot tree, he was happy.

In January 2008 we received a phone call from one of John's other daughters to say her and her boyfriend wanted to move to Barrow, and could they stay with us until they found a place of their own. We told them that of course they could and that they would be very welcome. So they arrived very soon after to stay for a while. John's other daughter and her partner came through one day to visit us and so now I had met all of John's five children.

It was on with the wedding plans and we arranged the date for the wedding. It was to be August the 8th, 2008. Unfortunately Morrisons would not let me have that date off work, so we had to change it to the 28th of August, which was just as good.

As we had seven children between us, I thought the fairest way was for each of our youngest daughters to be bridesmaids. As Hayley had been my bridesmaid for mine and Bradley's wedding, it seemed fitting that Emma was going to be bridesmaid for me now. I took the two bridesmaids along to the bridal shop at the top of Cavendish Street to choose our dresses. Both girls chose the same dress, which was fortunate. They chose a lovely burgundy, fitted, strappy, long dress and they both looked simply stunning in them.

Now what colour should I go for? I was seriously running out of colours for my bridal outfits. I'd had red, white and blue. So the patriotic road was well and truly done. I decided, seeing as I was marrying my prince, that I should go for a royal colour. Gold. I chose a similar style to the girls' dresses and so having done that it was only the tiaras and shoes to sort out. And that was the outfits complete.

I felt a little superstitious and didn't want John to know anything about our outfits. I've no idea why, as it certainly never did me any good for my past three weddings; however, as luck would have it John chose a lovely brown suit with longline jacket and a gold waistcoat for him and his best man, Dale. We really were in tune. He asked me what colour tie they should go for and without giving anything away, I suggested burgundy.

The wedding plans were coming along. Although I had only one disappointment to endure and that was when my beloved mum and dad announced that they were not coming to our wedding. I held back the tears as they explained that they didn't want to leave their dog unattended all day because he was prone to destruction, plus they weren't keen on going out nowadays.

"Anyway, don't you think we've been to enough of your weddings?" Dad laughed. "We're sick of wedding cake."

I couldn't help but feel disappointed.

"You'll have a lovely day," he added softly.

The day before our wedding arrived and I finally met John's lovely dad, sister and brother-in-law. I felt very emotional as I watched a slightly older version of John walk up our front garden path. I now realised where John got his exceptionally good looks from. Sadly, John had lost his beloved mum and his older brother in years gone by so I never had the privilege of meeting them.

The white stretch limousine, which Emma and Josh had hired for us as a wedding present, pulled up outside the house on our lovely, sunny wedding day.

"Come on, it's here," Josh shouted up the stairs to us girls getting ready. He picked up the camcorder and started filming us all coming down the stairs one by one with silly grins on our faces, trying to act normally. John, Neil and Dale had left earlier to go for a drink so that we could finish getting ready, but Josh stayed to do the filming.

John's dad, Josh, four of our daughters and I got into the plush Limousine and the driver skilfully took us on a slow drive along to the Nan Tate building on Abbey Road, to where the Register Office was now. We arrived to find everyone waiting outside to see the Limousine pull up. There was my special friend, Verity, who had travelled up from Watford with her new husband, Daniel, along with Bart and Maisy, Tom and April, Gloria and Phil, Sapphire and Shane, Vera and Andy, the rest of John's children, his sister and brother-in-law, and of course Daisy, Ernie, and their son, Toby, along with lots of others. Daisy was to be my witness of course; this was fitting as after all she had kind of introduced John and me in the first place, and Ernie was very kindly going to take the photographs for us.

We all went into the Register Office and the ceremony began. Afterwards, when I had become Mrs Gillespie, everyone travelled up to the Lisdoonie Hotel for our reception, where the hotel owners and staff did us proud. Vera had made us a beautiful wedding cake and it stood there on the side table for all to see. The highlight of the afternoon for me was when during the speeches, my new father-in-law stood up and welcomed me into their family on account of my own dad not being there. I found this gesture touching to the extreme and let a tear slip from my eye with emotion.

For the evening we had a do at The Kill One club in Duke Street, where we danced our first dance to 'Always' by Bon Jovi. A couple that I worked with did the disco, pie and peas were put on and one of our artistic friends, Declan, decorated the room for us. All of our family, friends and work colleagues were invited and the whole day from start to finish was no less that absolutely perfect. We stayed the night at the Lisdoonie which was lovely.

To finish off the celebration, John and I went on honeymoon to Blackpool. We stayed at The Elgin Hotel and it could not have been better. On arriving there by coach, we went into the bar to have an arrival drink to hear the sound of one of my favourite singers.

"They must have known you were coming. They're playing an Elvis Presley record so they are," said John.

But as we went to sit down we realised that it wasn't a record playing but a man, obviously the entertainment for the evening, singing an Elvis song 'A Pocket Full of rainbows' from the film GI

Blues.

"I'm not an Elvis fan, but I do like this song," said John.

"Yes, it's one of my favourites too," I replied.

This was the night that Blackpool switched on the illuminations, and after walking along the front to see the wonderful display of lights and catching a glimpse of the pop group 'Scouting for Girls' who were switching on the lights this year, we went back to the hotel to watch the brilliant act of Ricky Aaron. First there was a quiz on which were questions about the sixties. We won the quiz and received a lovely little teddy bear, which now sits in one of my dolls' houses. As I collect dolls and bears this prize was very welcome. Ricky put on a fabulous show and we asked him if he would sing 'A Pocket Full of Rainbows' for us and told him that we had just got married.

"In that case, here's a wedding present," he said, and he handed us a CD of himself singing.

We also bought one of his DVDs. He autographed them both for us, and they remain one of our special possessions. After the show, we sat talking to Ricky and his manager in the bar until very late. This made our honeymoon very special.

Eventually, it was time to leave Blackpool and go home to begin our married life together. This most definitely was the start of the rest of our lives.

CHAPTER 25

Two months went by and one day, about an hour before I was due to leave for work, John and I were sitting on our sofa watching TV. Kim was asleep on my lap as usual, when suddenly Kim got up, turned around and started trying to bury her head in my side.

"What are you doing Kim?" I asked rhetorically. At that moment she collapsed and I picked her up and held her close as she gasped her last breath and died peacefully in my arms. We rushed her to the vets quickly, but I knew that there would be nothing that they could do. The bravest cat in the world had gone. I was inconsolable.

With Kim gone, George had decided that now, he was going to be the boss of this house and proceeded to let my little Holly know this. Sadly, it wasn't long before he was the only cat left in this house, as my beautiful Holly contracted lymphoma, cancer of the blood. The vet put her on very strong pain killers, but as she wasted away and started struggling to walk, the vet suggested that we do the right thing for her, as there was no cure for this awful disease. So we had to say a sad farewell to our pretty little cat. Unfortunately Holly was only three years old. Life was so unfair for some, and this fact simply broke my heart.

Emma and Josh had moved house recently into a larger house

on Greengate Street and one day we called round to see them to find Emma looking a little sickly and Josh wearing a huge smile on his face.

"Emma's pregnant," said Josh excitedly.

"That's wonderful," I replied immediately going over to my daughter to give her a big hug and kiss.

"Congratulations," said John shaking Josh's hand.

This was exciting news indeed.

Christmas came and went and New Year's Eve brought heartache for Hayley and Neil as they ended their relationship and went their separate ways. Hayley came to stay with us for a while until she found a flat of her own. She moved into a little flat in Church Street with her two cats, Elvis and Derek. We all helped her move and settle in.

It was 9th May 2009 when our beautiful grandson, Alfie, was born. Emma and son came out of hospital and we all went for a walk around town together on Alfie's first trip out in his new pram.

"So, are you going to be called nana or grandma?" Josh asked me.

"Oh definitely nana," I replied.

Josh got made redundant from his job, and so I got him an application form for Morrisons. He got a job there, so everything was fine again.

The following year flew by and Alfie was christened just before his first Christmas. Then the following May, his first birthday was celebrated at Dalton swimming baths. All the children went for a swim along with their parents as we prepared the hired room for the party afterwards. They all enjoyed themselves and Alfie received lots of presents.

Exactly one week later, my friend Joanne died at the age of forty-eight. She had been ill for a while but the news was nonetheless shocking.

Shortly after that I received a phone call from Josh.

"Glynis, it's just as well you've just got those bunk beds for your third bedroom."

"Why?" I asked, slightly puzzled.

"Because Emma's pregnant again," he replied.

"Oh, that's wonderful!"

We were thrilled, another grandchild on the way. I couldn't help hoping that they would have a little girl this time.

However, the elation soon ended when Emma and Josh split up. It came as a huge shock, I really thought that they would be together forever, but it wasn't to be. Josh left Emma pregnant and desolate to pursue other women, and shortly afterwards at work I told him exactly what I thought of his actions. Emma and Alfie came to stay with us for a while. Then a house came up for rent in Buccleuch Court a few doors away from us, and Emma and Alfie moved into it. We all helped with the move. Emma went through her second pregnancy in turmoil after the breakup of her relationship with Josh. I went with her when she went to the hospital for her scan, and we found out that she was in fact carrying a little girl. We were all delighted. Alfie was going to have a little sister.

It was 29th April 2011 when our little granddaughter decided to make her appearance. Only the wedding day of our future King was good enough for THIS little girl's arrival. Josh and I were with Emma at the hospital throughout the birth, when this flame-haired mini Emma by the name of Lilly popped into this world.

Six weeks later John and I travelled up to Scotland to attend the christening of John's granddaughter. The occasion was lovely, but on returning home we came down to earth with a bang, when the following morning I received a phone call from Ernie.

"Hello Glynis. I've got some terrible news. Daisy has passed away."

I didn't think I'd heard him right. That can't be true, I was only chatting to her a few days ago at work. Daisy had worked in the cafe at Morrisons and we had chatted regularly both at work and on our darts nights.

"No, I can't believe it, Ernie. She was fine when I spoke to her the other day just before we went away. What on earth happened?"

I was so distressed. How on earth must he and Toby be feeling?

"She had a heart attack last night. It was sudden. One minute she was there, the next she was gone," he said.

"That's terrible. I'm so sorry for your loss, Ernie. How is Toby bearing up?"

"Well, he's still in shock at the moment."

"Yes, of course. That's understandable," I replied.

"I'll let you know what day the funeral's on," he said solemnly.

"Thanks, Ernie. If there's anything we can do for either of you please let us know, won't you?"

"I will," he said.

This was a lady who had defied death by overcoming cancer in the past. To have her life taken after all that, was simply tragic.

The crematorium was jam-packed on the day of Daisy's funeral. It was very clear that my friend was extremely well loved. There wasn't a dry eye in the place as we all said a sad farewell to a wonderful lady, and one of my best friends. Quite a lot of us went back to The Cross Keys to raise a glass to her. This was the place where she enjoyed her weekly game of darts and would often dance her special dance to the sound of 'Tiger Feet' by Mud. We put this song on the Jukebox this day and reflected upon our times with wonderful lady.

It was 2012. My wonderful dad, as head of four generations had reached the age of eighty. Of course Dad being Dad, he wouldn't go anywhere to celebrate, so I asked Vera to make a cake for Dad in the shape of a train. It was a lovely cake and he was thrilled with it. We had a small celebration at Mum and Dad's house.

Later that year, Emma passed her driving test and her dad bought her a car. This made things a little easier for her, as she was able to get a part time job as a career, where a car was needed. Hayley had moved from her flat in Church Street to a house in Duncan Street, but the stairs were not ideal for her on account of her having epilepsy, so after having had her name on the council list for a few years, she was offered a ground floor flat in Abbotsmead Approach. It is a lovely cosy flat, and she is very happy there with her two cats.

This same year brought the sad death of our dear friend, Maisy. She was eighty-six and had the awful disease Alzheimer's. Both Maisy and Bart had moved into Kingsfield residential home as Bart had done his very best in looking after Maisy up until then, but the time came where he couldn't cope any longer. We had always visited them in Kingsfield every week, and will continue to visit Bart. They were married for sixty-two years and Bart will always miss her.

March 2013, and my lovely father-in-law reached the age of eighty. John and I travelled to Belfast for this celebration. The weather was bad and the snow was thick that month, so as the lights went out in the restaurant we ate by candlelight, which was quite enchanting.

CHAPTER 26

It was one week after my beloved dad's eighty-first birthday when he was diagnosed with Alzheimer's disease. He very slowly got worse, but thankfully never got that bad that he didn't know us.

"My memory's getting bad, love," he would say to me. "I have to write everything down or else I forget."

"Don't worry, Dad. We'll help you," I told him.

He would flash his wonderful smile and everything would seem ok. Except it wasn't.

"Will you sort everything out for me, love?" he asked me.

"You don't have to worry about a thing, Dad. Of course I will."

"I don't wanna put you to any trouble, love."

"Nothing is too much trouble as far as you're concerned, Dad. You've looked after me all of my life. Now it's my turn to look after you," I told him.

We applied for power of attorney so that I could take care of all his finances for him. However three weeks before Christmas my dad collapsed with an aneurism in his heart and he was taken to hospital. We all followed the ambulance up there and the doctor asked Mum and I to go into a side room where, along with a lovely nurse, he explained the situation.

"I'm afraid he won't survive this," he said gently. "I'm very sorry but he could go at any moment. There is nothing we can do for him."

We were so upset, but when we got back to Dad's bedside, he was sitting up and smiling. We phoned Auntie Sheila and Uncle Eric to tell them what had happened. They said that they would come straight away to see him. They stayed a few days and we all visited Dad every day as he became stronger and stronger.

"Well we are very pleased to tell you that he can come home," the doctor announced the day before Christmas Eve. "It's no less than a miracle. This almost never happens, but the aneurism seems to have sealed itself," he told us.

We were elated. My dear dad was coming home for Christmas. Fantastic.

All the arrangements were made by the lovely social worker, and a home help was put in place to come and wash and dress Dad in the mornings and to get him ready for bed at night.

"I'm much obliged to you," he would tell them.

Dad was extremely grateful for their help and he often told them so. Mum would make his meals, although his appetite disintegrated slowly over the weeks that followed and Dad got worse and worse again, until the day we all dreaded arrived. It was the 20th February 2014 when I received the phone call from Mum.

"Glynis, Dad's been taken into hospital again."

"We're on our way, Mum," I replied.

Emma happened to be with John and I at the time, and she drove us up to the hospital immediately, picking Mum up on the way. Emma dropped us three off at the hospital entrance and went to pick Hayley up. The nurse took us into the visitor's room and told us that Dad had actually died in the ambulance on the way to hospital, but they had managed to revive him. My spirits lifted for a moment until she added the next sentence.

"I'm very sorry but he's slipping away again. We don't think he will last long so we'll take you to be with him," she said gently.

I was inconsolable as the tears welled up and cascaded uncontrollably down my face.

When we arrived at his bedside, John went and got some chairs for us and we sat either side of him. Emma and Hayley arrived shortly afterwards. He was practically unconscious but it appeared as though he was trying to say something. I leaned over him to try to make out what he was saying, but I couldn't make out what it was. Maybe it was goodbye, we will never know. I held his hand, but the lump in my throat prevented me from speaking and I mouthed the words "I love you, Dad" as he slipped gently away from this world.

Without a doubt this was the worst moment of my entire life. In all of my travels, and my troubles, Dad had always been there to guide me. Whatever my problems, my dad had always known what to do. The rock in my world had gone.

You could have heard a pin drop in the silence, as we all sat with our own thoughts, reflecting upon Dad's life, until the doctor came in and solemnly pronounced him dead.

Procedures had to be maintained and as Emma took Mum and Hayley home, John and I waited to officially identify my dad's body along with a very tactful police officer. I still couldn't find my voice as I nodded the necessary response to the identification. I was distressed and this time, my dad couldn't make it better.

John is my rock now, and he proved this with his natural care and attention, gently guiding me home and helping me through my heartache.

I phoned Morrisons and between sobs, I told my personnel manager about my loss. She was marvellous and told me to take all the time I needed. The days that followed were a blur as Mum, John and I made all the arrangements for the funeral. We went along to the funeral parlour to see Dad for the very last time. The atmosphere in the room was tranquil as we stood around his coffin with our own thoughts. I touched his cold hand and the painful realisation that he was gone suddenly hit me. This was the final moment of seeing the face of my guardian angel, the person who had kept me safe and guided me for the past fifty-six years.

The day of Dad's funeral arrived and it was time to say a final sad farewell to my wonderful dad. Auntie Sheila and Uncle Eric had travelled over the day before. We had ordered sandwiches from Morrisons and John went to collect them in the morning. My work colleagues all asked John how my mum and I were, and I found that comforting. Then we went to Mum's house to prepare the rest of the buffet.

The hearse arrived, along with the Limousine to take us to follow my dad on his final journey. I caught my breath as I looked at the flowers that formed the word DAD, the bouquet from Mum and the train arrangement that Emma and Hayley had bought, along with other family flowers. I couldn't speak as we all travelled behind my dad. Emma squeezed my hand in reassurance as the tears stung my eyes.

We arrived at the crematorium to find Amy, my bridesmaid from years ago, Mum's neighbours and a crowd of my dad's workmates from the railway. I was very pleased that they had all come to say goodbye to my dad, and I know Dad would have been too.

Mum had wanted the minister of the Baptist church to lead the service. However I wanted to be the one to supply some of the words spoken, so I wrote a condensed version of my dad's wonderful life. In six A4 pages I told the story of my dad's journey through life, and although I would have liked to have read it myself, I couldn't due to my emotions being in turmoil, so the very nice minister read it out. I know Dad would have approved of this minister as he conducted the service perfectly. We all left the crematorium to the song 'I Did It My Way' by Frank Sinatra, Dad's favourite singer. That said it all really.

Afterwards we went back to Mum's house to drink a toast to my dad's life, and my cousin Saffron phoned us to see how we all were. The strangest thing happened though. As we all sat reminiscing in the large lounge of my mum's house, Dad's TV at the other end of the room, which he watched continually, suddenly switched on. I noticed it first.

"Who switched that TV on?" I asked.

Everyone looked towards the other end of the room to where the TV was blatantly lit up with life.

"No one did. There's no one down there," said Uncle Eric.

"Well that's odd," said Mum. "How did that happen?"

I walked over to it and switched it off. We were all puzzled. There seemed to be no explanation for this strange occurrence.

MAYBE IT WAS MY WONDERFUL DAD, HAVING THE LAST WORD. I would like to think so, but we will never know.

CHAPTER 27

The year is 2015 and I am heading towards fifty-eight years old. If I had to describe my life now in only two words, they would be the immortal words of Mary Poppins, 'practically perfect'. Practically, only because of the absence of my dear dad, and perfect, because apart from that, my life IS absolutely perfect.

Life at Morrisons is pretty good. I have the good fortune to work with a fantastic bunch of people. However arriving into work some days can be somewhat of a challenge on occasions, especially when I hear the awful words from my good pal Gemma.

"You're on the kiosk today, Glynis."

Gemma, a young, extremely cute blonde, always has a smile for all of her colleagues and customers alike and it is a constant delight to be in her company.

"Oh no," is usually my grumpy reply, the situation lifted by the fact that I will be working with Gemma.

However I do not work on the kiosk permanently now. Most days I work on either the checkouts or self-scan, and am perfectly happy on both. So I just love it when I am greeted by our supervisor Zoe with words I DO like to hear.

"Can you go on self-scan please, Glynis?"

Zoe, our raven-haired beauty has an abundance of patience

and time for everyone around her. It is a pleasure to be in her company for sure, and she is extremely good at her job.

"Yes, of course I will," I will reply with a smile.

Sometimes our gorgeous Kate will be supervising. Kate was supervisor when I first started at Morrisons but has changed departments a few times in between. However her wonderful calm nature reflects on us all as she always has time and patience for everyone alike and it is a constant delight to be around her.

"Can you go on checkout eighteen please, Glynis," are words I also like to hear from Kate.

Whatever checkout I am allocated, I will happily go to and begin our busy day.

Two friends I favour however, are Jillo and Barbara. Both wonderful ladies were also supervisors in the past. However Barbara has stepped down to checkouts due to reducing her hours now, and Jillo has moved to the plants department where she is much happier. We meet up in the canteen and catch up on any news most days. One thing is certain though, there is always a smile, a wave or a hug from these wonderful two friends whenever we see each other.

We have a new manager at Morrisons now, and on the day he started, as he shook my hand and introduced himself to me, I couldn't help but notice the similarity of this action when my wonderful manager Simon back at Kwik Save introduced himself in the same way. I am certain that another good manager is on the cards for sure.

Our customers here in Morrisons Barrow are a wonderful crowd and they generally keep all of us staff cheerful. They have a knack of turning a dull working day into a joyful experience, and in return all of the staff work extremely hard in order to give our customers the good service that they deserve.

There are only two things in this world that I am frightened of. Heights and wasps. It's not so much the height as the fact that I tend to get drawn over the edge, and wasps, well don't get me started on those evil little creatures in stripy jumpers. When they come flying towards me I will trample anyone down who may get in my way in order to make my escape, I'm ashamed to say.

I don't do much sewing nowadays but I have recently taken up knitting and have made a few items so far with the help of my mum and Barbara from work who have both produced some excellent knitting. I am still playing darts and can actually hit the dartboard on occasions, so everyone in the pub have even stopped ducking now, and I've gone on to win some trophies.

My precious mum, who looked after me so well along with my dad while growing up, has just moved into Buccleuch Court a few doors away from us, and my gorgeous daughter Hayley is not too far away. However the downside of this particular year is that my beautiful daughter Emma, my grandaughter Lilly and my grandson Alfie have just moved away to Kirkby Stevens. It's only just over an hour's trip so it could be worse, and this happens to be the right move for her at this moment in time. As we have all had to make these choices in our lives, Emma has to do the right thing for her, and this is it. She has met a very nice chap and is going to be with him. She even has a good job to go to, but Emma has assured me that we will still see a lot of her, so I am consoling myself with that thought. Josh, Alfie and Lilly's dad, is about to go into the Army so he accepted Emma's move as he is not going to be around anyway. Although the past four years since Emma and Josh split up have not always been easy, with us acting as go-between for most of it, passing the children from one to the other through us; however their differences seem to have been put to the side now and everything is running smooth between them at last. Josh will visit the children in Kirkby Stevens whenever he has some leave.

Of course I miss my dear dad and there is never a day goes by that I don't think of him. But I have a lovely life now and am extremely happy with my wonderful, gorgeous, clever, extremely considerate husband John. Unfortunately it did take me almost fifty years to find him, but sometimes one has to kiss a lot of frogs to get one's prince, I understand.

I don't see a lot of my auntie Sheila, uncle Eric or my cousins Saffron, Juliette and Pricilla, but we all keep in constant contact and we know that each other is ok.

I have been lucky enough, along the way to accumulate a number of very good friends. Someone once said to me many years ago when I was young, "Glynis, as you go through life you will meet a number of acquaintances along the way, but you will only be able to count on one hand the amount of true friends you will have in the whole of your lifetime." I, however would have to take my shoes and socks off to count the amount of true friends that I have.

I consider myself to be extremely lucky as John and I have a comfortable life, both working part time, we have a comfortable home, keeping in touch with all of our family and generally enjoying life. I think it's safe to say, it doesn't get any better than this. I remember my dear dad saying to me on my dark days that the path of life never runs smooth for any one of us, and along the way there will be ups and there will be downs, so when a person reaches rock bottom, well, the only way left to go is up. As I reflect upon my life from past to present, I realise that it has been quite a roller coaster ride, but a wonderful journey. FROM THE GARDEN TO THE LAKES.

FROM THE GARDEN TO THE LAKES